The West Wing

TV Milestones

THE WEST WING

Janet McCabe

TV MILESTONES SERIES

Wayne State University Press   Detroit

17 16 15 14 13   5 4 3 2 1

Library of Congress Cataloging-in-Publication Data
McCabe, Janet.
The west wing / Janet McCabe.
p. cm. — (TV milestones)
Includes bibliographical references and index.
ISBN 978-0-8143-3436-2 (pbk. : alk. paper) —
ISBN 978-0-8143-3809-4 (ebook)
1. West Wing (Television program) I. Title.
PN1992.77.W44M44 2012
791.45'72—dc23
2012018533

CONTENTS

v

I would like to thank The British Academy, for supporting this project with a Small Grant Award.

Those who have read and provided helpful criticism of this book in manuscript form have been essential to its thinking and rethinking. I am particularly indebted to Kim Akass, Stacey Abbott, and Deborah Jermyn for advice and encouragement in the initial stages. In addition, Michele Hilmes and Philippa Brewster offered invaluable comments on sections of this work.

I am grateful to Stefania Carini and Joana Amaral Cardoso. I also extend my deepest gratitude to Eli Attie, Dermot Horan, head of acquisitions and scheduling at RTÉ, and Francesca Ginocchi, communications director at NBC Universal Global Networks Italia, for giving generously of time and answering my questions with patience and clarity. This book has benefited immeasurably from their input, for which I am truly indebted.

I want to take this opportunity to express my gratitude to the readers of the manuscript and editors of the TV Milestones Series, Barry Keith Grant and Jeannette Sloniowski, for encouraging me to clarify my ideas, as well as streamlining the prose and improving the work. In addition, Annie Martin, acquisitions editor at Wayne State University Press, has shepherded me with unfailing support and become a good friend along the way, as well as Jennifer Backer for her sterling efforts in preparing the final manuscript.

As usual, I owe a colossal debt to Mike Allen, for his wise counsel and help with the images while I furrowed my brow. I also thank him and Olivia for giving me enough space to write this book.

Politics of Quality U.S. TV

All the President's Men . . . and a Few Good Women

NBC had high hopes for its brand-new behind-the-scenes ensemble drama about Washington politics. Premiering on 22 September 1999, *The West Wing* was the most eagerly anticipated U.S. network show of the fall season (competing alongside forty-two other freshman series). The show certainly had pedigree. Its cast featured Martin Sheen and former Brat Pack movie star Rob Lowe, its subject matter was ambitious and germane, and its production team included John Wells, executive producer of *ER* (1994–2009), and Aaron Sorkin, creator of the short-lived but critically acclaimed *Sports Night* (ABC, 1998–2000) and author of *A Few Good Men*, for which he had received an Oscar nomination.

Four years earlier, Sorkin had scripted the romantic-comedy *The American President* (Rob Reiner, 1995), about widowed president Andrew Shepherd (Michael Douglas) falling in love with lobbyist Sydney Ellen Wade (Annette Bening). As the story goes, Sorkin wrote more than 385 pages for the 120-page screenplay and refused to discard the surplus (Rayner 2005). The following year his agent arranged for him to meet with Wells. "I knew . . . the moment I sat down . . . he was expecting me to pitch something," recalls Sorkin. "So it suddenly occurred to me: what about senior staffers at the White House?" (Weinraub 1999a, 4). With the "little shards of leftover stories" from *The American President* Sorkin wrote the TV pilot of *The West Wing*.

A month after delivery, in January 1998, the Monica Lewinsky scandal broke. NBC held back the project, sensitive to the political mood and suspecting that viewers had little appetite for a show about Washington politics (Hoffmann 2000). Salacious revelations and an impeachment hearing made the network cautious about the viability of a White House drama at a time of so much political rancor; as Wells explains: "[NBC] said they couldn't take it to the advertisers in that climate" (Graham 1999). Sorkin, in the meantime, went to work on *Sports Night*, about an ESPN-style network. But with charges against President Bill Clinton dropped in February 1999 and a regime change at NBC, "the unthinkable happened," writes Sorkin. "Somebody forgot to tell Scott [Sassa, president of NBC West Coast] and Garth [Ancier, president of NBC Entertainment] you can't do a show about Washington and politics" (2003a, 6).

At the show's core is a team of dedicated senior staffers: shrewd beltway veteran and chief of staff Leo McGarry (John Spencer); deputy communications director Sam Seaborn (Lowe) (replaced in Season Four by the equally talented Will Bailey [Joshua Malina]); press secretary Claudia Jean "C. J." Cregg (Allison Janney); communications director and conscience of the administration Toby Ziegler (Richard Schiff); deputy chief of staff Josh Lyman (Bradley Whitford); and personal aide to the president Charlie Young (Dulé Hill). Donnatella "Donna" Moss (Janel Moloney), Josh's able assistant, replaced political consultant Madeleine "Mandy" Hampton, PhD (Moira Kelly) as a series regular in Season Two.

Originally intended to be a peripheral figure, President Josiah "Jed" Bartlet (Sheen)—the intellectually formidable former New Hampshire governor and liberal Democrat, Nobel Prize–winning economist, and descendant of a Declaration of Inde-

The Bartlet team

pendence signer—proved so popular that he soon moved center stage. Recurring characters like First Lady Abigail "Abbey" Bartlet (Stockard Channing) and younger daughter Zoey Bartlet (Elisabeth Moss) as well as vice presidents John Hoynes (Tim Matheson) and later Robert "Bingo Bob" Russell (Gary Cole) joined the cast of a series about a fictional Democratic White House charged by highly principled but flawed individuals striving to govern honorably.

The West Wing began in the closing years of the Clinton administration (1993–2001), a post-Lewinsky era of political scandal and partisan vitriol. Aspiring to turn around the deep cynicism pervading American political life, the series "went for nobility and for politics with a purpose" (Bianculli 2000). It combined the representation of the quotidian with high-minded governance and debated weighty political questions alongside stories of its all-too-fallible characters. Its visual pace was kinetic, its dialogue smart and witty. Only a Steadicam could hope to keep up with the numerous plots involving staffers dashing through the labyrinthine corridors of power at impossible speeds. Each week the show provided a vibrant civics lesson on a broad range of issues from hate-crime legislation and gun control to budget appropriations and the arcana of U.S. Census sampling. Constitutional law and domestic policy intertwined with foreign affairs as the administration dealt with Middle East discord and the specter of international terrorism (centered on the fictional Qumar).

What started as a hopeful take on government as a noble calling or, as Sorkin put it, a "valentine to public service" (Carter 2006, E7), found its creative niche, for better or worse, by evoking a parallel political universe as America lurched rightward with a Republican administration under George W. Bush (2001–9). In this alternative world where life and politics mimicked the real world but rarely collided with it, the Bartlet administration struggled for political survival—creatively and commercially. Always "a precarious juggling act," claims critic Noel Holston, the series was "a lifelike fantasy both dependent on and vulnerable to events in the real world" (2001b, B2).

"Truth was more immediate than fiction," wrote Lance Parkin about the series as it struggled to adapt following the terrorist attacks on American soil in September 2001 (2006, 46). Put simply, cataclysmic world events seemed more compelling than anything *The West Wing* could ever imagine post-9/11. A discernible shift from representing internal Washington politics to stories involving terrorism and foreign tensions could soon be detected. Republican voices grew louder, and crises increasingly drove the presidency. Bartlet may have spoken as a social liberal, but he often behaved like a hawk on the major issues, especially those involving international affairs and the military. Set against a real U.S. presidency obsessed with homeland security and mired in a contentious foreign conflict, and a country split by the schismatic cultural wars, *The West Wing* lived in the divide between its liberal idealism and the nation's conservative reality.

Season Six saw a reshuffle. New faces and fresh crises redefined the Bartlet presidency, while Josh, Donna, and Will (temporarily) left the White House for the campaign trail. Plots increasingly focused on the hotly contested presidential election: primaries, debates, and party conventions included. Topical debate about important issues returned, something that had set the show apart from the very beginning. The presidential race was primarily carried out between Democrat congressman Matthew Santos (Jimmy Smits) and Republican senator Arnold Vinick (Alan Alda), with a potential third candidate, vice president Robert Russell.

The seventh and final season closed in 2006 with the inauguration of America's first Hispanic president—the youthful, charismatic, but unseasoned coalition-building newcomer who talked impassionedly of change and hope. What at the time seemed awkwardly contrived and faintly implausible became remarkably prophetic when Barack Obama became the forty-fourth president of the United States in January 2009. It has been widely reported that the writers modeled their presidential hopeful on the senator from Illinois. Even so, the show prefigured with astonishing accuracy the 2008 presidential campaign: the long and bitterly fought clash of Hillary Rodham Clinton against Obama, a Republican ticket mired in entrenched ideological schisms, and a "pro-choice" Republican nominee with appeal beyond the conservative base (only to be held back by it). Somehow *The West Wing* looked relevant again, as having something of vital importance to tell us about our political, historical, and cultural epoch. Time had thus served to skew our sense of this show as significant.

Judging the milestone status of any television show is a precarious business. There is something inherently difficult about initiating such a debate, even while acknowledging that it should be undertaken. On what basis are judgments made?

In identifying why this primetime ensemble drama deserves its TV milestone status, this book situates *The West Wing* within broader debates about television and cultural worth related to U.S. culture and quality TV (Thompson 1996; Jancovich and Lyons 2003; McCabe and Akass 2007). The volume seeks to discern the ways in which *The West Wing* was part of a complex agenda that worked hard to tell us that NBC's political drama was, to adopt Robert J. Thompson's definition of quality TV, "better, more sophisticated, and more artistic than the usual network fare" (1996, 12).

There is, dare I say, a political impulse at stake here. Charlotte Brunsdon said it best when she wrote: "there are always issues of power at stake in notions such as quality and judgement—Quality for whom?, Judgement by whom?, On whose behalf?" (1990, 73). Propelling such an argument is the sense that we must be acutely aware of the grounds on which judgments about quality are being made—and this is invariably political. Every cultural product is deeply invested in the political character of its society, for this is what precipitates it and gives it vibrancy. Thus, in revealing *The West Wing*'s specific political provenance—its production, its creative pretensions, and the rhetoric surrounding it—a discussion about what constitutes *a politics of quality TV* forms the backbone of this contribution.

If, as Jane Feuer states, one definition of quality is "cultural relevancy," "to capture the 'feeling' of a culture undergoing change" (1984, 8), then *The West Wing* created a "feel" for its time. The line between fact and fiction, news and entertainment, often blurred; in 2002 NBC repeated a *West Wing* episode following a documentary special titled *The Bush White House: Inside the Real West Wing*. Featuring NBC news anchor Tom Brokaw, the documentary chronicled the inner workings of the executive mansion post-9/11, but, more significant, the Bush White House came across as being strangely similar to the finely crafted fictional one (Bumiller with Rutenberg 2002). Elsewhere, cataloguing the real-life counterparts of the principals (Hillary Rodham Clinton/Abbey, George Stephanopoulos/ Sam) preoccupied commentators, and cast members mingling with professional politicos made the news, as did Sorkin's hiring of political experts as creative consultants. A whimsical poll taken during the 2000 presidential campaign found that 14 percent of those asked would vote for Bartlet (Parry-Giles and Parry-Giles 2006, 170). There were even "bumper stickers [promoting] . . . 'Bartlet for President' and the Green Party . . . [asked] Sheen to become the running mate of Ralph Nader" (Conrad 2000, 2). *The West Wing* generated buzz, it energized its audience, and it ignited genuine debate. Like it or loathe it, the series touched a cultural nerve with a language and verisimilitude that somehow spoke of the post-Watergate, post-Lewinsky, post-9/11 political condition.

Questions of verisimilitude dominated the critical and press reception of the show. *The West Wing* was praised for its realism while simultaneously condemned for being "nothing more or less than political pornography for liberals" (Podhoretz 2003, 223). The show was disparaged and acclaimed in equal measure—commentators fiercely debated its political relevance in a divided critical reception paralleling partisan party politics. Peter Rollins and John O'Connor (2003) took a more philosophical approach in a collection that assessed *The West Wing*'s contribution to film and history; how the series reimagined the U.S. presidency and recalibrated the American political consciousness determined how others, like Melissa Crawley (2006) and Trevor Parry-Giles and Shawn Parry-Giles (2006), interpreted the show's cultural and ideological significance.

"*The West Wing* is one of the dramas, like *Hill Street Blues* [NBC, 1981–87] and *NYPD Blue* [ABC, 1993–2005], that pushed forward the concept of television and drama," observed Brad Adgate, senior vice president and director of research at New York–based Horizon Media. Of its legacy he remarked that the show "took television in a different direction" (Garron 2006, 188). Explaining exactly what is meant by "new direction" in television is perhaps not so easy, for there is always something notoriously elusive about describing the new. Nevertheless, the risk taken with *The West Wing* proved sufficient enough that at first NBC took charge of what made its new political series unique. Evoking ideas of quality in terms of authorship, stellar casting and acting (associated with legitimate theater), high-production values, and the latest television image-making technology, upscale viewers and serious high-minded (political) debate helped distinguish what made *The West Wing* stand out as a beacon in the highly competitive television marketplace. Such a concept of culture includes a refining and elevating element, of making visible, as Matthew Arnold put it in 1865, the best that has been known and thought within a particular society.

Offering close textual readings of selected episodes drawn from all seven seasons to illuminate the above, this book investigates how the critically acclaimed White House drama series interrupted the television "flow" to provide a space for a vibrant political conversation about U.S. politics, identities, and culture, as well as TV storytelling, televisuality, and the institution of contemporary television.

Politics of Quality Primetime TV

Network Politics and Broadcasting Context

NBC always seemed quietly confident that *The West Wing* represented the best of what was possible on the network. With its big cast, big ideas, big investment, and big profits, the series soon proved a powerful asset to its broadcaster as well as the company that produced it, Warner Bros. Television. This chapter addresses institutional importance and how the primetime, Washington-based drama legitimized TV fiction and its trading, both at home and abroad. It explains why the U.S. network invested substantial monies in licensing and marketing the show, how it scheduled it, and how, in turn, demographics and industry awards as well as international broadcast territories contributed to sustaining an institutional idea about *The West Wing* as important quality TV. Studying the media history reveals that the multi-Emmy-award-winning political primetime series mattered because it mattered to those who mattered. What sustained the network's eagerness to keep *The West Wing* in its schedules (even as ratings plummeted), how NBC and Warner Bros. Television managed and institutionalized the show as about prestigious quality TV drama, has something important to tell us about broadcasting politics in the age of TVIII[1]—an era driven by, among other things, brand equity and customer choice, locating "quality" demographics, and defining niche television markets.

NBC, Democracy, and the Politics of U.S. Network Broadcasting

The West Wing may have ushered in new ways of representing politics in television drama, but its language for doing so remained deeply implicated in ideas about broadcasting philosophy and corporate identity. Milestone TV programs promise to somehow liberate television from what went before, but, to borrow from Todd Gitlin, "In network television, even the exceptions reveal the rules" (1994, 273). In comprehending how NBC institutionalized markers of quality *in* and *through* its broadcast agenda and company values is crucial to understanding, in part, what made *The West Wing* stand out in a competitive television landscape.

The West Wing circulated free-to-air on the NBC network. The series thus belongs to a longer tradition of U.S. public broadcasting that stretches as far back as 1926 with its origins in radio. Toby, in fact, reminds network news directors of that history—of how the federal government gave the publicly owned airways to the networks for free seventy years earlier and how they, in return, had an FCC (Federal Communications Commission) obligation to legally serve the public ("The Black Vera Wang," 3:20). Michele Hilmes writes that NBC positioned itself as "America's network" hinged on principles of "social diversity and cultural standardization, . . . national integration and local independence, and . . . First Amendment–protected freedoms and the need for regulatory control" (2007, 8). These tensions between competing ideologies, in turn, subtly shape the decision-making broadcast philosophy governing the network, a central conflict between "public service responsibilities and . . . [its] commercial economic base" (ibid.).

From lessons on the planet Mars ("Galileo," 2:9) to identifying the only three words in the English language beginning with the letters "dw" ("Mr. Willis of Ohio," 1:6), *The West Wing* had a predisposition to the conditions of public service broadcasting. It was a philosophy embedded in the dramatic conversational forms, as well as explicitly referenced as a theme or plotline. Asked by the president to free up five appointments to the Corporation for Public Broadcasting, Toby, as the voice of uncompromising social liberal idealism, sees it almost as a personal crusade to protect PBS ("Take Out the Trash Day," 1:13).

> Toby: I was raised on *Sesame Street*, I was raised on Julia Child, I was raised on *Brideshead Revisited*. Their legacies are safe in my hands.
> *C. J. unable to curb a snigger.*
> Toby (*to C. J.*): You got a problem?
> C. J.: You watched cooking shows?
> Toby: I watched Julia Child.

Audiences expect nothing less from Toby. But he is not alone in acting as a guardian of public service values. C. J. accepts the challenge to debate on live television with conservative talk-show host Taylor Reid (Jay Mohr), as she is keen to put forward an opposing argument and restore political balance ("An Khe," 5:14). Later C. J. crusades for the independence of local news affiliates against media conglomerate buy-ups ("Talking Points," 5:19). Abbey even gets to film a public service announcement, in which she gives the *Sesame Street* character, Elmo, a health check ("Eppur Si Muove," 5:16). This sense of public service broadcasting celebrated in the series speaks *about* television as being independent enough to actively participate in the democratic process, educating while it entertains.

How NBC's public service remit entwines with pragmatic business interests also had an impact on what constituted political balance on the show. Despite always having a decidedly liberal skew, voicing oppositional argument remained deeply

11

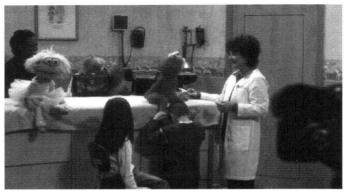

Abbey gives Elmo a health check on PBS

lodged within the show's distinct dramatic and visual structure. Debate involved embracing a wide variety of different opinions and oppositional views and reflected NBC's institutional commitment to reaching the broadest audience possible. Moving into Season Two, when it looked likely that George W. Bush would take the White House in November, producers searched for Republican script consultants. Marlin Fitzwater, former press secretary to Presidents Ronald Reagan and George H. Bush, and Peggy Noonan, former speechwriter and special advisor to Reagan, were subsequently recruited as advisors. In the 2002–3 fourth season, with ratings on the slide, the commercial instinct was to steer the show in a more conservative direction (Holston 2002). NBC apparently urged Sorkin to alter the political tone, sensing that characters were far too liberal for a nation drifting to the right (Petrozzello 2002; Murphy and Schwed 2003, 39). Switching from a Democrat to Republican president in the dying moments of the Season Four finale appeared to herald a potential ideological shift; Alessandra Stanley noted how "some fans of the show" interpreted the move as "a sly political statement—an effort by NBC to curry favor with the real powers that be" (2003b, E6). The dramatic denouement finds Bartlet invoking the Twenty-Fifth Amendment. He temporarily abdicates rather than risk allowing personal anguish to cloud his political judgment following the abduction of daughter Zoey ("Commencement," 4:22; "Twenty Five," 4:23). With the vice presidency vacant (because of a sex scandal), next in line is the Speaker of the House, Glenallen Walken (John Goodman), a bellicose Republican who brings a strong dose of hard-line conservatism to the White House. Walken occupied the Oval Office for only a few episodes in Season Five, but (hawkish) Republican voices remained forever present— from characters like Ainsley Hayes (Emily Procter) and Arnold Vinick to the behind-the-scenes appointment of Fitzwater and Noonan as political consultants to the show. Sorkin reportedly never clashed with the network over the politics, and the series went "out of its way to present all sides of issues ranging from school vouchers to the Middle East" (Weinraub 2000, E8). Attempts to balance political debate (however problematic) not only staved off accusations that the show had too liberal a slant, which had the potential to estrange viewers and sponsors alike, but also referenced a model of broadcasting tailored for public benefit.

Speaking on a panel titled "Hollywood Goes to War? Politics, Showbiz and the War on Terrorism" in December 2001, Sorkin declared: "I hope the biggest thing [foreign audiences] get is that we can do whatever show we want" (Gerber 2002, 73). This is a bold pronouncement about creative freedom and artistic integrity. Given that the U.S. network is a commercial medium, profoundly dependent on advertising dollars and the vicissitudes of the free market, what is meant by "creative freedom" is nonetheless determined overwhelmingly by *how* the American television business operates. Several times NBC has judged it good business sense to sponsor television drama that defied conventional network wisdom. Dominant media institutions like NBC are perpetually being influenced and trans-

13

formed by ways of thinking about and producing television drama that have been developing elsewhere in the cultural landscape. In the early 1980s, NBC took a risk with *Hill Street Blues* as the network suffered something of a commercial and creative slump. Throwing away the TV rulebook and taking a chance on something different looked nothing less than the smartest thing to do for a broadcaster struggling as the third-ranked network. In a relatively short span of time, predicated partly on the critical acclaim the police precinct series received, NBC recovered much of the ground it had lost to commercial rivals, especially in the prestigious area of drama.

In recent times, nothing approaches the degree of free expression and artistic advantages enjoyed by premium pay-to-view cable channels like HBO. When *The West Wing* premiered in 1999, HBO was fast gaining a reputation for pushing the envelope on program content with groundbreaking and critically acclaimed original shows like *Oz* (1997–2003), *Sex and the City* (1998–2004), and *The Sopranos* (1999–2008). Without advertising pressures or strict limits on content, HBO made a virtue of its autonomy from that which constrained network television. The channel's concentration on a few high-profile series reflected a pragmatic business move to meet the fresh challenges facing the industry. The ratification of the Telecommunications Act in Congress in 1996 was intended to grant as much economic latitude and content freedom to the industry as possible; it paved the way, notes Hilmes, for deregulation and "sparked a tsunami of corporate mergers" (2003, 66). HBO's program output may have had a clear sense of direction rooted in this legislative change, but the subscriber channel belongs to the same media conglomerate as the company producing *The West Wing*, Warner Bros. Television. Far from competing, *The West Wing* was never really in direct competition with the HBO originals as much as it represented another asset in the Time Warner media portfolio.

Commissioning practices, regulatory agencies, and broadcasting standards bodies do define, for better or worse, the possibilities as well as limits of free speech on network television. Soliciting reactions to why *The Sopranos* drew critical acclaim and strong ratings, Bob Wright, president of NBC, sent a memo to TV network executives in 2001, asking "whether there is a lesson in there for NBC" without specifically imitating the HBO series or offending NBC viewers and alienating sponsors (Carter 2001a, C7; Carter 2001b). Wright's communication betrays vexation at how the public network is subject to more stringent controls than the pay-cable channel, particularly in relation to representing sex and violence and the use of profanity. Sorkin even spoke of the constraints affecting the way he tells a story. "If *The West Wing* were on HBO . . . President Bartlet could say, 'Fuck' during a tirade. On HBO, we probably wouldn't have cast someone as handsome as Rob Lowe, and the hooker [Laurie Rollins played by Lisa Edelstein] he gets together with wouldn't be a Georgetown law student with a heart of gold but a hundred-and-fifty-dollar hooker from the book. But I tend not to write like that" (quoted in Friend 2001, 89). Despite Sorkin's claim that production restraints do not necessarily affect the way he writes and regardless of how broadcast limits are constantly being challenged, broadcasting standards do condition, define, and regulate what can and cannot be done when producing network drama.

Further, such broadcast practices have led to a perception that networks fail to handle shows with the same kind of integrity as do the cable channels. TV critic Adam Buckman identifies the predicament. He starts by praising the second season finale when President Bartlet stands before the altar of the National Cathedral and denounces God—in Latin ("Two Cathedrals," 2:22). Grieving the senseless loss of his trusted secretary Dolores Landingham (Kathryn Joosten) and struggling to make sense of his own past, the president calls the Almighty a "sonofabitch" and "a feckless thug." "It's a challenging monologue," Buckman writes, "deeply moving, beautifully written, marvelously acted, and bound to be controversial" (2001a). Buckman was not alone in drawing attention to this extraordinary scene (Zoller Seitz 2001, 31), testifying to its impact as something rarely attempted on network television. However, Sorkin admits in the "Constructing Two Cathedrals" bonus featurette that the decision to put the tirade into Latin was less a creative choice than a pragmatic one. Using Latin enabled him to get the language past the network censors and avoid any potential controversy over the way in which Bartlet reproaches God.

Referring to Wright's 2001 memo, Buckman further identifies why viewers abandoned network television for cable channels like HBO. The reason, for him at least, had nothing to do with the quality of shows like *The West Wing*, which in his opin-

Bartlet stands before the altar in the National Cathedral

ion was "the best drama on broadcast television" (2001a), or because NBC was restrained by traditional broadcast standards, but because of certain devices that the networks use "far too often and should stop doing" (ibid.). Cliffhangers, for example: the network should respect viewers and trust them enough to return for the next season without resorting to such ploys. Other vexing elements include "the length and frequency of commercial breaks, which are making TV shows ever more difficult to follow; the insanity of midseason reruns resulting from the fact that there are too few episodes to fill a season anymore; and the increasing use of on-screen billboards for upcoming shows" (ibid.).

No doubt these complaints about network interruptions compromising textual integrity have grown ever more audible within the American context since channels like HBO have trained our attention so closely onto the text. Evoking this idea of network television as somehow undermining originality with contrivances and constant disruptions undoubtedly serves HBO well; it allows the cable network to rationalize its scheduling practices and broadcast philosophy (thirteen episodes, telling stories differently and with no interruptions) while loudly proclaiming to have raised the creative bar by doing what the commercial networks cannot.

Nevertheless, it is precisely because of these factors governing the politics of network television that the caliber of *The West Wing* comes into view. "This is a show broadcast TV needs to see succeed," wrote TV critic Diane Werts. "Without the language, violence and sex of *The Sopranos*, Sorkin's *West Wing* proves it's possible to do incisive adult drama while staying within traditional network standards" (2001, B3). The series was ambitious enough to be judged against its own aspirations and creative ingenuity rather than against what else existed in the television landscape.

NBC, *The West Wing,* and the Politics of Quality Primetime TV Drama

TV series dealing with politics often meet with suspicion from network executives, and *The West Wing* was no exception. So worried was NBC that the series nearly did not make it on the air. "The old regime at NBC was very concerned about the show," Sorkin said, "because, in general, politics tends to be a turnoff for people" (quoted in Garron 2000, 104). The series may have boldly led the way into uneasy primetime territory, but it did so because NBC got serious about the politics. The network sold the difficult subject matter as challenging adult drama with a sophisticated sense of humor and did so *in* and *through* its distinctive channel brand, which is, as Amanda Lotz describes, "leveraged in promotional slogans such as 'the quality shows on NBC' and 'must-see TV'" (2007, 262).

Even before its debut, *The West Wing* was the 1999 fall season's most hyped new series. NBC gambled on its success, promoting the show heavily since the spring. The network scheduled its brand-new political drama in the coveted primetime time slot, 9:00–10:00 PM on Wednesdays (where it stayed until Season Seven when it was shifted to Sunday evenings). *The West Wing* was placed in what Warner Bros. Television president Peter Roth claims is "arguably the most competitive time period on [American] television" (quoted in Lowry 2002). For, as Lotz explains, primetime dominance "affords the most cultural cachet" (2007, 263).

Quality TV has long had something of a reputation for needing time to find its audience (Thompson 1996). It is a perception enshrined in network practice, which works hard to pick up viewers and turn drama, in which a broadcaster has invested heavily, into appointment viewing (i.e., when viewers set aside time to watch a particular show). NBC built an audience for the political series during the summer of 2000 when many (including me) first saw the show in rerun. Furthering that interest, the network inserted advertisements for the upcoming second season during September coverage of the Sydney Summer Olympics, reinforcing NBC's reputation as a reliable brand of distinctive, quality programming. No preview tapes were made available to avoid spoilers. No one talked to the press ahead of time. The network instead escalated anticipation for the second season, scheduled to start Wednesday 4 October at 9:00 PM, with incessant promos, asking "Who's Been Shot?"—Season One had ended with the Bartlet team coming under a hail of bullets while leaving a town hall meeting in Rosslyn ("What Kind of Day Has It Been," 1:22). Canny scheduling strategies and aggressive marketing campaigns enabled NBC to create a "buzz" for the show. It laid the ground for what Sorkin called "The momentum of word of mouth [which] finally lit the fire" (quoted in Weinraub 2000, E8). As a result, the two-hour-long Season Two opener was the most-watched show in primetime with a 16.3 share, which translated into twenty-five million viewers (Combined News Services 2000). This figure was up from the previous year, when *The West Wing* ranked thirtieth among network shows, with an average weekly audience of fourteen million. The crucial idea is that milestone television in contemporary times *is* appointment television, the assumption being that discriminating remote-clicking viewers *only* make room in busy schedules for must-see programs.

Closer inspection of what NBC did with its freshman drama over that summer also gives further insight into how scheduling practices serve network interests politically. NBC reran four stand-alone episodes timed to coincide with the party convention season, but, as identified by Eric Mink, the NBC strategy had "another timely political dimension to it" (2000). This was the week when the Emmy Awards panel met to assess nominees. Despite official voting protocol stipulating that judgments can only be made based on submission tapes and that "[general] impressions of a series' performance, promotional ads taken out by the producers and networks—even a strategically scheduled on-air flurry of a given series' episode—are supposed to be ir-relevant," the "concentrated burst of *West Wing* episodes, the on-air promos touting those episodes and whatever additional press attention the episodes generate can't hurt the show's chances in the judging process" (ibid.). Intended or not, on 10 September 2000, *The West Wing* walked away with an unparal-leled nine Emmys, including Outstanding Drama Series—an accolade it claimed for the next three years.

Substantial investment in the beltway ensemble drama translated into profit and industry recognition. In its freshman year alone, and including its haul of Emmys, the show secured the Humanitas Prize, a Peabody Award for excellence in televi-sion, a Golden Globe nomination for Best Drama Series, and three Television Critics Association Awards. It increased its tally and at the end of the second season added the Directors Guild Award, Producers Guild Award, Writers Guild Award, and Screen Actors Guild Award to the list. The show also became only the third series ever to win a second Peabody.

The West Wing enjoyed strong popularity over the next two years, increasing its audience share during Season Two against the real-world backdrop of the bitterly contested 2000 presi-dential election. The series climbed to the top of the ratings alongside *Friends* (NBC, 1994–2004) and *ER*, and tied, midsea-son, for fourth with CBS's family-based sitcom *Everyone Loves Raymond* (1996–2005). *The West Wing* hit its popularity peak in the third season (2001–2), when it ranked tenth in the ratings with a weekly audience of more than seventeen million (Buck-man 2006).

The West Wing was always conceived of as a prestigious high-profile corporate investment. Replicating a senator's office cost $80,000 to build, and in 2001 episodes were priced at around $2.7 million to produce (Waxman 2001, B3). Power comes from being a market leader—and Warner Bros. Televi-sion was in a strong negotiating position. The production company brokered a good syndication deal (especially given that television drama historically fails to repeat well) with the cable channel Bravo, selling rerun rights for $1.1 million per episode (Kaplan 2002). John Wells further acknowledged that despite high expenditure and budgetary deficit, negotiations between NBC and Warner Bros. Television over licensing rights would see the network paying "several times the current sum to continue airing the hit" (Waxman 2001, B3).

Its position was so strong that *The West Wing* even managed to survive unwelcome headlines and several end-of-season crises, beginning on 15 April 2001 with Sorkin's arrest for drug possession at Burbank Airport and concluding with the actors' strike in July, when four cast members—John Spencer, Allison Janney, Richard Schiff, and Bradley Whitford—walked out over pay disputes (Kaplan 2001). Eventually contracts were renegotiated, and the series entered its third season with its quality network assets—its ensemble cast and principal series writer— intact and a second Emmy for Outstanding Drama. Economically *The West Wing* was worth the trouble; and with thirty-second advertising spots reportedly selling at around $293,000, the ad gross per show provided NBC with revenue of $5.8 million.

Two years later, the series' "blockbuster credentials" and prolonged durability did not seem as guaranteed as they once did. In its fourth season, and despite winning its time slot, *The West Wing* started to lose ground in the Nielsen ratings, posting its lowest numbers since it first began in 1999. Rob Lowe quit. Sorkin resigned. Thomas Schlamme followed close behind. Worse still, viewing figures continued to drop, especially among the all-important age bracket of eighteen- to forty-nine-year-olds. Ratings experienced a modest rebound in Season Six, as the arrival of new characters injected fresh life and new candidates. Nonetheless it was not enough to reverse the show's sliding political fortunes. In its seventh and final season, *The*

West Wing ranked only eighty-third, with less than 8 million still watching. Even the live presidential debate, with an estimated 9.6 million viewers, was not enough to challenge ABC's supremacy on Sunday evenings. So, in January 2006, and in the wake of Spencer's fatal heart attack, NBC announced that primarily because of declining ratings it had decided not to renew the series.

The question as to why NBC chose to keep one of the most expensive shows in primetime on air for as long as it did found those with any measure of authority endlessly justifying the financial worth and critical importance of the series. In 2003, although *The West Wing* was displaying vulnerability, NBC decided to renew its licensing agreement with Warner Bros. Television, settling on a fee of $6 million per episode. Part of that deal also involved keeping the rights to air the series on NBC for another two or three seasons (Battaglio 2003). Despite reports that "the formal negotiations [were] as intensely political and fractious as anything seen in the fictional White House" (Carter 2002), it was an extraordinary settlement for a struggling show. President of NBC entertainment at the time, Jeff Zucker explained: "Obviously *The West Wing*'s performance is not what it was a year ago, but *it still remains the best show on television*" (quoted in ibid.; emphasis added). Network willingness to back a creatively challenging show that is no longer a strong ratings performer says much about how investing in a particular program is about more than economics. It helps raise the profile of a broadcaster, guaranteeing clout in the marketplace as a purveyor of prestigious television. Taking charge of what made *The West Wing* unique, inserting the series into a system of value, enabled NBC to manage a reputation for itself. In time, the knowledge and reality created by what exactly that might mean established criteria by which *The West Wing* as quality landmark TV was commercially determined.

Vox Populi, Vox Dei: Locating the "Quality" Demographic

Guiding NBC's programming philosophy in the late 1970s, executive vice president of programming Paul L. Klein advocated his theory of "least objectionable programming" (LOP). He believed that viewers stayed tuned unless somehow startled. "Thought, that's tune-out, education, tune-out" (1979, 17). Politics fell into this category. Commercial television has long been cautious about commissioning political dramas amid fears of distancing viewers and driving away sponsors. The Bartlet team was forever vigilant of polling data, but networks like NBC are no less interested in the figures.

Klein may be better known for his LOP philosophy, but he also championed the belief that demographic categories (rather than sheer numbers) were more useful indicators of a show's success for advertisers. NBC reversed its fortunes in the early 1980s by commissioning distinctive dramas like *Hill Street Blues* and *St. Elsewhere* (1982–88) aimed at a viewership the network could sell to sponsors at higher rates. In 1981, replacing Fred Silverman as NBC chairman and CEO, Grant Tinker "institutionalize[d] the philosophy of reserving some slots in the schedule for upscale programming" (Thompson 1996, 67). With *Hill Street Blues* proving "a workable model whereby literate and complex drama could be made for prime-time television" (74), the ambition to produce targeted programs for a "smaller, 'quality audience'" (67) instituted a commercial philosophy of quality *The West Wing* later embodied.

Early ratings indicated that *The West Wing* audience "skewed fairly old" and that it "was especially popular in larger markets like New York and Washington" (Weinraub 1999b). This was the crucial upscale demographic earlier identified but had in recent times been perceived as drifting to niche cable channels like HBO. When *The West Wing* first aired it went up against *The Drew Carey Show* (1995–2004), the popular ABC comedy that owned the time period, and CBS's strongly performing movie night franchise, along with WB's highly anticipated high school/ alien teen drama *Roswell* (1999–2002) and the much-hyped drama *Get Real* (FOX, 1999–2002). Tough competition certainly, but *The West Wing* held strong in its time slot. Strategized as smart adult counterprogramming leading into *Law & Order* (1990–2010), *The West Wing* helped boost the NBC brand "as the network of 'upscale,' college-educated, eighteen- to forty-nine-year-old viewers" (Lotz 2007, 270).

NBC executives never failed to mention how the political drama delivered a disproportionately high number of affluent, upwardly mobile, better-educated, urban-minded professionals, ranking first among primetime shows in the percentage of eighteen- to forty-nine-year-olds boasting a median income of $75,000 and above (Carter 2002; Huff 2002; Lowry 2002). One can never claim that appeal for *The West Wing* reached much beyond that niche, but the network's grasp on that valued "quality" audience whose viewership was used as leverage in negotiations with advertisers proved crucial.

Ratings for *The West Wing* peaked in the 2001–2 season but thereafter fell steadily. ABC's new reality TV dating show, *The Bachelor* (2002–present), with its 12.8 million viewers, helped siphon away the younger demographic (women in particular). In the fourth season, and running opposite strong competition from *American Idol* (FOX, 2002–present), *The West Wing* saw its audience dwindle from 17 to 14.9 million (Battaglio 2003), reduced further in Season Five to 11.7 million (Weinraub 2004, E1). Even with this precipitous drop in the ratings, the political drama continued to deliver the most elite audience of any primetime show. This made its commercial time an exceedingly attractive buy for advertisers, especially clients such as Lexus, Mercedes, and BMW, looking for high-skewing shows (Huff 2002). Securing premium rates from sponsors, the show's value lay in its delivery of a coveted but often hard to reach demographic with high-end consumer habits, which, in turn, persuaded NBC to retain the series despite the gradual ratings slide (Carter 2003a).

Formulaic maybe, sentimental and schmaltzy at times, but with its adroit use of language and rhythmic cadence, crackling wit, and political savvy, *The West Wing* had its audience craning "forward to catch the dialogue" (Kramer 1999). As Werts writes, the series "asked a lot of its viewers from the start" (1999). With minimal action—no medical emergencies, no police chases— the ensemble drama placed extraordinary emphasis on smart vocabulary and quick-witted verbal exchanges that made few concessions to the audience. The LOP philosophy of TV viewership was thus replaced with the idea of a discerning viewer discriminating enough to tune in and smart enough to keep up.

Serious issues require serious-minded viewers: it was an elitist attitude toward watching—and thinking differently about—television. As Arlene Hellerman explains, "Rather than preaching particular ideas, the characters on *The West Wing* engage in dialogue that compels the television audience to engage in thought" (2003). At the end of an episode in which staffers try to get the Comprehensive Test Ban treaty to the floor, Toby tells the president that all is lost ("The Lame Duck Congress," 2:6). Bartlet respects the treaty opponents but says he "couldn't give a damn about what the people think." Given the complexity of international treaty agreements, 82 percent of the general public cannot possibly "be expected to reach an informed opinion" on it. Yet the implied message was that those watching *The West Wing* can. Able to understand the complexities of the geopolitical world and receptive to pluralistic ideas, the imagined audience for the series was implicitly positioned, both in the text and beyond it, as that elite 18 percent able to follow intricate political argument.

Keeping up with the politics as well as fast-paced banter required more than rapt concentration and attentive listening. It required another look. Once, only the most avid fan would archive every single episode of a favorite show—not any lon-

25

ger. Investing time now translated into investing quite literally in buying the series, first on video and later DVD. *The West Wing*, repackaged in these ways, finds income-rich, time-poor viewers able to run their own "appointment-to-view" diaries. Owned, sometimes without necessarily being watched, the collector's box set sits on shelves alongside novels, music, and film titles, sending out important messages about what we culturally invest in. Just as Bartlet relishes handling an 1886 first edition copy of *The Fables of Phaedrus*, with red leather label complete with gilt lettering and an engraved frontispiece ("In Excelsis Deo," 1:10), *The West Wing* on video/DVD is parceled to display aspiration. These objects are quietly fetishized as bold statements about personal preference, consumer habits, and a canon of contemporary taste. *The West Wing* on video/DVD, like *The Fables of Phaedrus*, is perceived as having cultural cachet, as something worth possessing, further justifying why viewers should make room for this exceptional series on their shelves.

The New Imperialism: International Sales and Foreign Markets

"The world hates us, and even Americans deplore the sorry state of political discourse in their country," wrote Alessandra Stanley. "But only the uninformed or disingenuous complain about the quality of American television. It has a variety and breadth that no other nation can match" (2005, E1). U.S.-acquired programming has long played a role (however large or small) in foreign territories. In recent times, though, with twenty-four-hour schedules voracious for content and channels seeking survival in a highly competitive marketplace, imported American content has increasingly helped overseas broadcasters stay ahead of rivals. For example, RTÉ in the Republic of Ireland directly competes with U.K. broadcasters like the BBC and Channel 4 in its home market. "The trick is," says Dermot Horan, head of acquisitions and scheduling at RTÉ, "to be the first run" (2010). Shows like *The West Wing* enabled the Irish broadcaster, which was the first European TV station to air the series, to stay ahead of the cultural curve and define its institutional importance.

The West Wing arrived in the U.K. as a multi-award-winning series. The show debuted in September 2000 on Sky One, Mondays at 9:00 PM, before filling the vacancy left by *The Sopranos* on the digital subscription channel E4, where the dramatic two-part Season Two opener, "In the Shadow of Two Gunmen" (2:1, 2:2), premiered on 19 June 2001. As in other non-U.S. territories, the British broadcasting context reveals the deal with Warner Bros. Television (rather than a network), showing how primetime U.S network programs are often scheduled alongside niche cable ones: *The West Wing* was followed by *Curb Your Enthusiasm* (HBO, 2000–present), *Friends* before *The Sopranos*. Such scheduling enables minority public channels like Channel 4 to build their brand and a corporate reputation precisely by bringing the best in American acquisitions to British television (McCabe 2000).

The West Wing later helped launch the new U.K. digital channel, More4, in October 2005. British audiences had waited almost an entire year before the sixth season aired. Eagerly anticipated, its eventual return helped lure audiences to the new channel. *The West Wing* aired every Friday night in a regular peak-time 9:00 PM slot, with first-run episodes running consecutively for ten months as the sixth segued into the seventh season. The show's inclusion in the More4 schedule also helped deliver the agenda for the new channel, defined by its head Peter Dale as embodying "the values that [Channel 4, the parent company] had held dear since it started—independence of thought, a delight in taking risks and a passion for the new" (2005). The adult entertainment channel had a decidedly political edge, branded as seeking "to reclaim territory for free-thinking, open-minded grown-ups who wanted to be challenged as well as entertained" (Channel 4 2005). Its official public-

27

ity document, sent out free to homes across the country, had Bartlet in a tuxedo center stage—an image that also appeared on billboards and the sides of buses. From political satire with *The Daily Show with Jon Stewart* (Comedy Central, 1996–present) and high-profile documentaries adopting a strong political stance to the news program *More4News*, sustained debate, balanced argument, and critical analysis dominated the channel—and *The West Wing* with its discourse of complex issues became reimagined at More4 as part of its corporate identity dealing with contemporary, often challenging and controversial political topics.

Before moved to More4, where it found its niche, trying to find the series in the U.K. schedules often proved a frustrating business. The show was subject to erratic scheduling, betraying a cultural anxiety about U.S. imperialism: a tension of dominant American/global forces against national public service broadcasting policy and "local" interests. In the Republic of Ireland, the public broadcaster experienced similar pressures. *The West Wing* originally aired on Thursdays, at 10:15 PM, before being pushed later into the night until it secured an 11:15 PM slot—far from its primetime location on NBC at 9:00 PM. Irish TV critics may have complained, even blaming Horan personally (Horan 2010), and despite RTÉ taking pride in having *The West Wing* in its schedule, the public broadcaster could never air the show in primetime. Because RTÉ is publicly funded to serve Irish citizenry and facilitate domestic production, the broadcaster has always had difficulty justifying foreign acquisitions. Funds raised from the license fee must be primarily spent in primetime; otherwise questions are raised. *The West Wing* aired only once, but it "claimed its space" in the RTÉ schedule, predicated on being a prestigious and important acquisition for the Irish broadcaster.

Although it never rated as high as Horan had hoped, *The West Wing* found a select yet loyal audience among ABC1 adults living in metropolitan areas. It was a demographic profile repeated across Europe. Correspondence with Francesca Ginocchi (2010), communications director at NBC Universal Global Networks Italia, confirms a similar trend in Italy. Given that the series aired on both pay and free-to-air commercial Italian channels meant that NBC Universal Italia could run the series in primetime, at 9:00 PM, with three repeats throughout the week. As such, *The West Wing* was perceived as a "high-end" first-run show (ibid.), an elite product for an elite cosmopolitan audience. Moreover, in continental Europe, where language is a major factor, that demographic narrows even further. Ginocchi readily admits that "the subject matter and language of the show could not attract a wider [Italian] audience," but *The West Wing* remained an "important" and "classy" series for them (ibid.). Essentially, the show was dubbed but with the option to see it in the original, which, of course, required a sophisticated grasp of English. Given the density of the language delivered at a brisk pace, the series never did good business in territories where subtitling predominates, like Scandinavia and the Benelux countries (Horan 2010), raising further questions about U.S. cultural imperialism as well as the uncompromising nature of *The West Wing* text. As it was in the U.K., so it was elsewhere—the series asked much of its "quality" audience.

Chapter 2

Politics of Storytelling and the TV Auteur
Authorship, Performance, and Narrative

Bringing new levels of stylish wit and intelligence to prime-time television defined *The West Wing* as exceptional. Credit for its complex plots, intense characterizations, and linguistically dense dialogue went, more often than not, to series creator Aaron Sorkin. In a medium like television, where the producer traditionally reigns supreme, writers are rarely so esteemed; but recognition "transformed . . . Sorkin from a *wunderkind* into an institution" (Downing 2005, 135). His proficiency at scripting dialogue with such striking narrative rhythm hardly ever heard before on network TV and the way he "carefully crafted and jealously guarded each word" (Garron 2006, 188) was endlessly recycled in the press and critical literature (see Fahy 2005). Sorkin may have ushered in an original kind of rhetorical style, but he did so, as this chapter asserts, using language and narrative forms deeply implicated in concerns regarding American national and cultural identity. This fundamental link between discourse and identity led to a sense that *The West Wing* was somehow alive to something in the political air but also determined why the series became so privileged within contemporary U.S. popular culture—and survived even after Sorkin left the show.

La politique des auteurs: Sorkin as TV Auteur

"I love writing but hate starting," Sorkin writes. "The page is awfully white and it says, 'You may have fooled some of the people some of the time but those days are over, *giftless.* . . . I'm a white piece of paper, you wanna dance with me?' and I really, really don't" (2003a, 3). Still, start writing he did. Putting in seventeen-hour days. Seventy pages of dialogue per week. Crafting, rewriting, and polishing each line. Eight-six episodes. Four seasons.

Or so the story goes.

Long before Sorkin severed his connections with the series, the popular perception was that he dominated "the writing process in a way unheard of on team-based shows such as *Friends* or *The Sopranos*" (Burkeman 2003, 2). As Thomas Fahy remarks, "We don't think about the team of writers . . . or the staff generating story ideas for *The West Wing*; we think only of Sorkin" (2005, 2). Words like "brilliant," "gifted," "maestro," and "genius" were routinely used to describe him, while Adam Sternbergh called Sorkin "TV's reigning savant of spitfire dialogue" (2006, 72). This idea of Sorkin as having ultimate authority over the script invests *The West Wing* in the kind of authorship long associated with other privileged cultural forms: theater, international art cinema, and literature. Authorship in these terms is a relatively simple idea, essentially referring to someone with an uncompromising personal vision. Just as *Cahiers du cinéma* bequeathed to film criticism "an essentially romantic conception of art and the artist . . . art [transcending] history, expressing man's freedom over destiny" (Hillier 1985, 6), behind the authorial-based critiques is a similar logic applied to network television.

"With references to Shakespeare and Graham Greene, visits to rare-book stores and oblique Latin episode titles like 'Post Hoc, Ergo Propter Hoc,'" writes Peter de Jonge, "the show is so achingly high end that you almost expect the warning 'Quality Television' to start flashing below the picture" (2001, 46). This seeming encyclopedic engagement with literature and language grounded *The West Wing*'s bid for respectability within already established debates about creative worth, but it was in the constant assertion of Sorkin as sole arbiter of the script that compelled us to think that way. Privileging the writer in this way grants legitimacy based on hierarchies of cultural taste and value (Bourdieu 1984). Proclaimed through media profiles of Sorkin (see Sternbergh 2006) and pursued in aggressive marketing campaigns and ancillary publications like the script books with transcripts of selected episodes with commentaries by Sorkin (Sorkin 2003a, 2003b), authorial intent defined this primetime network drama as innovative and rewarding—justifying its status as appointment to view.

The evocation of the TV auteur as having more or less a free hand to tell stories in whatever way he chooses also raises questions about the role of the head writer working in contemporary network television. Traditionally imagined as a "conveyor belt" system, writing for network television has long had the reputation for being relentless and subject to restrictive broad-

Author-in-the-text: Aaron Sorkin

cast practice. It is, however, those very conditions that allowed Sorkin to thrive. That sense of him, with his acute mental agility, writing at a "breakneck speed," preparing scripts in only eight days, producing a weekly primetime network drama full of intricate dialogue spoken by uncommonly clever characters dashing through the corridors of power, became central to *The West Wing* mythology. Comparing Sorkin with David Chase (creator of *The Sopranos*) as "the difference between the work of a bona fide pro and that of an inspired amateur," Jeff Zucker said, "Look, Aaron gives us 22 episodes a year, not 13, and he gives it to us at a schedule that we set" (quoted in de Jonge 2001, 47). In praising Sorkin, Zucker reveals a lot about the creative pace dictated by stringent production and television schedules. The truly gifted artist transcends these prosaic commercial concerns, whereby the precocious writer with an extraordinary talent for scripting dialogue emerges not only to rationalize a way of producing network TV drama but also as an undisputed category through which the quality of that work can be arbitrated.

Sorkin may have been judged the genius behind the series, but disputes over writing credit jeopardized the auteurist label. Trouble started at the Emmys in 2000 when, on accepting the award for best script, Sorkin did not give Rick Cleveland, his cowriter, the opportunity to speak. What added to Cleveland's irritation was that the "In Excelsis Deo" (1:10) episode had been based on the experience of his father, a Korean War veteran who ended up an alcoholic living on the streets. Cleveland was so aggrieved that he recounted his humiliation in an article for the *Writer's Guild of America* magazine, *Written By* (2000). Sorkin retaliated with a less than flattering Internet posting, followed by a profuse apology after Cleveland complained. The incident did not quite end here but instead prompted further grumblings from former writers about Sorkin's reluctance to share writing credit (de Jonge 2001, 46). Critical adulation turned to backlash following more unwelcome headlines concerning a disagreement involving staff writers over contracts and more unflattering press about him monopolizing the limelight.

Over budget and often behind schedule, *The West Wing* was, by 2003, in trouble, despite the fact that NBC had renewed its deal with Warner Bros. Television. There were missed deadlines, escalating costs, and highly paid actors left standing around waiting for scripts. "Sorkin's penchant for turning in pages at the last minute sent *The West Wing* $3.8 million over budget this season. No small sum for one of the most expensive television shows to produce," reported Mary Murphy (2003, 38). Authorial excess and workaholic habits are fine as long as viewing figures hold steady. "It's hard to imagine," Brian Lowry remarked, "Sorkin being badgered about late script delivery and related budget overruns had viewership stayed aloft. . . . After all, such excesses are more easily excused as the cost of dealing with an 'artist' when the payoff is unbridled success" (2003).

West Wing staff writer and later producer Eli Attie described how the writers' room functioned under Sorkin.

> Generally, the staff would come up with . . . story ideas without Aaron, we'd pitch him what we had, then he'd give us feedback . . . and ultimately we would write up our pitches and give him written material from which he would cull each scene. He very much wrote and shaped the vast majority of scripts, but from a lot of smart, heavily researched material from a very hardworking staff. And, of course, people like myself and Dee Dee Myers were on hand to provide political jargon and twists and thematic concepts unique to that world. Anything we pitched or wrote or suggested, Aaron would sprinkle his magical fairy dust on and make it great. There were also a handful of scripts written by other writers, particularly Kevin Falls and myself in the fourth season, which Aaron would then polish and/or rewrite. (2010)

Sorkin's abrupt exit changed everything. By the time the series returned for its fifth season, John Wells was in charge of the writers' room. He was the series' third producing partner and one of U.S. TV's most powerful writer-producers with credits including *China Beach* (ABC, 1988–91), *ER*, and *Third Watch* (NBC, 1999–2005). Wells may have confessed to "feeling daunted" (Carter 2003b, E1), but the change of creative guard signaled a break from the centralist practices of Sorkin. The writers' room shifted from a kind of absolute monarchy to a democracy, as "the show became truly multi-writer" (ibid.) and staff writers were no longer simply pitching storylines and preparing drafts. Although they received feedback from Wells, senior staffers like Attie, Paul Redford, and Debora Cahn started to control and produce the episodes they wrote. "Whereas, under Aaron," Attie recalls, "we were writing the show he wanted to write, and only that, John was more interested in making it democratic—steering the ship, but having a bunch of key writers who could share in the decision-making, and tell the stories we wanted to tell as well" (ibid.).

Given the way in which Sorkin had controlled the writing process, his departure left Wells with a problem. As Attie explains, "The plain fact is that many of the writers on the staff had never written an episode that was aired in any form" (ibid.). Just as truly the best and the brightest were called to serve at the pleasure of President Bartlet, Sorkin hired smart and hardworking people—but "without regard for whether they could actually write good scripts of the show" (ibid.). The writers' room had been "a place of solitary confinement"; as Wells remarks, "it became very important for [Sorkin] to write or rewrite every episode" (Garron 2006, 188). Once Sorkin had gone, Wells said, "it was inevitable that the voice of the show would have to change because Aaron was that voice" (quoted in ibid., 190). Wells replaced most of the writers (except for a few like Attie). He streamlined production and brought in a new staff of experienced TV writers, including Carol Flint (*ER*) and John Sacret Young (*China Beach*). This was a different, more collaborative process, but nonetheless these names were associated with quality mainstream network television.

A Few Good Stories: Structuring Drama and the Narrative Style

The West Wing was a standard primetime network TV series: a weekly hour-long show, twenty-two episodes per season, a four-act set piece with formulaic structure, a workplace drama with ensemble cast, filmed at a Hollywood studio. It was about, as Michael Wolff describes, "what television is about: quickly formed relationships, hurried intimacy, sharp language, everyday dysfunctions, tense, emotional negotiating, juicy human failings and foibles" (2000, 45). In this, the series perhaps, offered nothing unique.

The West Wing nonetheless employed dramatic principles more commonly associated with legitimate theater than network television. Initially conceived of as echoing postmodernist plays like Tom Stoppard's absurdist tragicomedy *Rosencrantz and Guildenstern Are Dead* (1966), the series centered on lesser characters working "in the wings" of the grand stage with brief appearances from the more important ones. But storytelling protocols also referenced older theatrical canons (e.g., Aristotle and Shakespeare) and included a complex use of language that had absorbed lessons from respected twentieth-century American playwrights such as Tennessee Williams, Eugene O'Neill, and David Mamet. *The West Wing* juggled high-stakes political drama with comedy, epic theater with dialogue crafted for effect. A "feeling" for presidential power took shape through intimate characterizations, and the series used language like musical notation with a rhythm, clarity, and image all of its own.

Season Three started properly (following the last-minute insertion of the 9/11 special) with a two-parter titled "Manchester" (3:2, 3:3). It begins where the second season ended, with Bartlet seeking reelection, and traces the buildup to his official announcement. Staffers, struggling to absorb the news of Bartlet's multiple sclerosis, strive to craft the reelection message. Doubts, mistakes, and concerns start to creep in, and these two episodes do what *The West Wing* did best: dramatize individual struggles and personal conflicts beneath the official machinations of presidential power.

Antipathy over how best to manage the campaign runs high between Toby and Doug Wegland (Evan Handler), a consultant hired by Bruno Gianelli (Ron Silver). Lying beneath the acrimony for Toby, at least, is his indignation over what the president has done. Toby is, above all else, a New Deal Democrat. Government must be a force of good and effect change for the better. His deeply held principles *are* his politics; the fact that Bartlet is concealing a serious health issue is a personal affront to him. It temporarily affects his ability to do his job. Doug knows it. Toby knows it.

C. J. also struggles after a major press gaffe ("Manchester: Part 1," 3:2). Tired and assailed by questions about the president's health, she responds to a simple question about Bartlet's authorization of peacekeeping troops to be sent to Haiti with, "I think the president is relieved to be focusing on something that matters." The briefing room falls silent. It is a huge faux pas for a woman whose genius lies in her ability to spin a story with finesse and stylish wit. She never misspeaks. "Damn it." Josh also tries to amend for an earlier miscalculation. Known for his hubris (which is often played for laughs), and despite being counseled otherwise, he coerces a Republican subcommittee to give the Justice Department another $30 million to fund its lawsuit against the tobacco industry ("The Fall's Gonna Kill You," 2:20). As a consummate political operator, Josh gets the job done but gives the anti-tobacco issue away. Bruno tells him that his vanity has cost them three crucial swing states—Pennsylvania, Michigan, Ohio—and political leverage against the Republicans in the upcoming campaign.

Individual brilliance, personal loyalties, private ethics, human foibles—these highly principled characters are often seen "doing the 'wrong' thing for the 'right' reason" (Fahy 2005, 3). It is in the intense interior drama involving smart, overachieving, but deeply flawed individuals, struggling with conscience while serving at "the pleasure of the president," that political ideas and ideals are given a passionate voice. It is also in the individual commitment to those principles that what the Bartlet presidency stands for primarily comes into view.

The approach taken by Sorkin and described, while also practiced, by Attie when structuring the drama was "to write thematically—to have a big idea, and throw various story threads into the mix that all relate to that idea, or comment on it from different angles" (2010). Dispersing a theme through different subplots and weaving them into a coherent narrative whole defined the structure of each episode. For example, in "Hartsfield's Landing" (3:15), war games is the subject du jour—from the pranks practiced by Charlie and C. J. on each other to the chess matches the president plays with Sam and Toby, from Donna and Josh engaging in retail politics in the tiny New England town of Hartsfield's Landing with its forty-two registered voters to the high stakes of international brinkmanship, as the Chinese conduct military maneuvers in the Taiwan Strait.

In the episode, Bartlet gives Toby a chess set with which Lord Louis Mountbatten, the last Viceroy of India, played India's first prime minister, Jawaharlal Nehru, in 1947. The players' topic for tonight, however, is not India's independence. Neither is it the crisis in Kashmir nor the free elections in Taiwan (all issues discussed elsewhere in the episode). It is reelection and the Bartlet psychosis. Pieces get moved around the board and humor eases initial tensions. This is the first time the warring pair has met since their quarrel resulting in Bartlet's epic bout of sleeplessness. The president says that his therapist blames Toby for bothering him. "I forgot for one second that you were hilarious," Toby replies. The stakes start to escalate; and in a twist whereby Toby doesn't play as well as he might, he tells Bartlet with deep political conviction and rhetorical inflection that the president doesn't have to act "plainspoken." "Make this election about smart, and not," he declaims. "Make it about engaged, and not. Qualified, and not. Make it about heavyweight. You're a heavyweight." Beat. "And you've been holding me up for too many rounds." Toby drops his king.

Alongside this match is a lesser one with the more inexperienced Sam. This contest is about teaching strategy and the rules of brinkmanship. Of course Bartlet wins, both the match and his war games with China. Sam gets beaten. But it matters not, for the deputy communications director learns important lessons about diplomacy and military tactics. How well (or not) each man plays speaks of their abilities to strategize, while the episode offers a good example in plotting action according to the articulation of a themed (political) argument, as well as the pacing of a dramatic rhythm for how that debate might sound.

Sliding back and forth in time motivated by subjective states of mind—trauma, memory—proved another dramaturgical

Bartlet and Toby play chess

feature. Flashbacks are central to the 2000 Christmas episode when Josh is diagnosed with post-traumatic stress disorder following his near-fatal wounding at Rosslyn ("Noël," 2:10). Initially antagonistic, Josh is now uncooperative. A flashback takes us to a time three weeks earlier when a brass quintet performed in the White House lobby. Dr. Stanley Keyworth (Adam Arkin), in the present, urges Josh to think harder, but he only deflects. A sudden knock at the door triggers his memory. He is dressed in white tie and his hand is bleeding. Time shifting continues with Keyworth pushing Josh to remember and he unable to do anything but relive the experience. Yo-Yo Ma playing the Bach Suite in G Major at the congressional Christmas party is heard by Josh as gunshots. Music gets translated into screams and sirens as he lives through the shooting again in his mind. Just as music prompts time shifts to convey lingering psychological scars, shards of half-heard conversations, church bells chiming, Bible readings, and Mozart's *Requiem* help Bartlet retrieve a repressed memory in another episode ("Two Cathedrals," 2:22) as he decides whether to seek reelection. As the president delves deep into his personal history, what he remembers of the past reaffirms his political purpose in the present—and sets in motion a new storytelling cycle.

Flashbacks were also used in the "Manchester" two-parter. Picking up immediately from where the previous season ended, the story develops with dual storylines, moving back and forth between Bartlet's initial declaration that he will run for a second term to the staff four weeks later preparing for the official campaign announcement. This time shifting engenders disorientation in the viewer, as it registers the bewilderment of senior staffers scrambling to get ahead of the news cycle in the wake of the president's announcement about his MS. The team tries to move forward and build an effective campaign while struggling to come to terms with the news. Memories thus serve an important function for narrative catharsis and individual healing; remembrance gives psychological depth and fills in backstories while the retelling of the past creates narrative closure in the present.

"Oratory Should Blow the Doors Off": Language, Conflict, and Performing Dialogue

Network television drama has long favored static studio spaces emphasizing the spoken word, but *The West Wing* took this formula to new dramaturgical heights. Describing the show's language, Clive James wrote, "the frantically energetic inhabitants speak modern American English in its highest state of colloquial eloquence" (2003, 18). It is no small coincidence that several of its principals were on the communications staff—Toby, Sam, and (later) Will, crafting the political message in stump speeches, the State of the Union Address, and the Inaugural Address. These men grappled with syntax, worried about cadence; they searched for language equal to the historic moment and talked of how, as Sam proclaimed, "oratory should blow the doors off" ("The Portland Trip," 2:7).

Quick-fire repartee pacing the action and crafting language for effect became the show's trademark. Allowing plots to unfold through conversation is "a stage technique that Sorkin developed as a playwright" (Wells quoted in Starr 2003). Graduating from two-act plays to the four-act structure of the TV series, Sorkin brought to television a unique way of scripting dialogue: pure verbal action, arcane styled phrasing, the energy and exuberance between two characters debating until the point is exhausted. Put simply, *The West Wing* told complex stories *in* and *through* the quality of language.

"This is fundamentally an office show where nothing really happens on the screen," Lawrence O'Donnell Jr. said. "It probably violates every television convention" (quoted in Weinraub 2000, E8). Given this distinct lack of action, *The West Wing* relied heavily on extracting the inherent drama from political discourse, sometimes on the most unlikely of subjects like the banking bill ("Enemies," 1:8), mandatory minimums ("Lies, Damn Lies, and Statistics," 1:21), estate-tax law ("Ways and Means," 3:4; "On the Day Before," 3:5), capital gains tax ("Disaster Relief," 5:6), and even government procedurals, such as appointments to the Supreme Court ("The Short List," 1:9; "Separation of Powers," 5:7; "The Supremes," 5:17) and the filibuster (the right to unlimited debate) ("The Stackhouse Filibuster," 2:17). International affairs also sparked impassioned argument—trouble in Haiti ("Manchester," 3:2, 3:3), a coup in Venezuela ("Process Stories," 4:8), genocide in equatorial Africa ("Inauguration Part 1," 4:13; Inauguration Part 2: Over There," 4:14; "Red Haven's on Fire," 4:17), and a hostage crisis in Bolivia ("365 Days," 6:12).

Week after week, visitors came to the White House to debate various topics, from C. J. taking a meeting about a wolves-only highway ("The Crackpots and These Women," 1:5) to a lecture on the politics of the Indian subcontinent from Lord John Marbury (Roger Rees) ("He Shall, From Time to Time . . . ," 1:12). In the final two seasons, the series hit the campaign trail where the candidates stumped on a range of policy issues while the Bartlet administration brokered peace between Israel and Palestine ("NSF Thurmont," 6:1; "The Birnam Wood," 6:2) and intervened in Kazakhstan. Nothing was ever simple: there were never un-nuanced answers, only complex weighty issues requiring sharp minds and smart thinking. Hence talking through appropriate courses of action drove narrative exposition; and spirited dialogue involving conflict and dispute, disagreement and consensus, shaped political verisimilitude. As Leo tells Jordan Kendall (Joanna Gleason) on the night Bartlet wins his second term in an election landslide: "The process matters more than outcome. And that's what we wanted. And here endeth the lesson" ("Process Stories," 4:8).

"The various sides of a political argument," wrote Arlene Hellerman, "are less important to [Sorkin] than the process of crafting words into an active debate" (2003). Adroit wordplay delivered with a precise rhythmic cadence defined how the politics was communicated, particularly in the first four seasons. *The West Wing* always demonstrated a deep commitment to articulating opposing political views, for this is where the "feeling" and passion for political principles lay. In "The Drop-In" (2:12), Bartlet asks Lord Marbury where he stands on the nuclear missile defense shield Leo favors.

> Marbury: Well, I think it's dangerous, illegal, fiscally irresponsible, technologically unsound, and a threat to all people everywhere.
> Bartlet: Leo?
> Leo: I think the world invented a nuclear weapon. I think the world owes it to itself to see if it can't invent something to make it irrelevant.
> Marbury: Well, that's the right sentiment. And certainly a credible one from a man who's fought in a war. (*Music swells.*) You think you can make it stop. You can't. If we build a shield, somebody'll build a better missile.

As in this brief exchange, and illustrated elsewhere in the series, scenes were driven by this kind of verbal confrontation.

It was, however, in the delivery of the words where the drama truly thrived. It was in the style of utterance, how the actors altered pace, tone, or rhythm, slid down the words and hit others—the inflection, the emphasis, and the pauses. In the above exchange, the polished English vowels of Rees (a leading Shakespearean actor) clash with the textured, gravelly tones of Spencer, as both make representation based on a weight of experience. In giving impassioned voice to a particular position, characters are shaded: the intellectual, slightly effete philosopher-diplomat at home with royalty and political dignitaries, and the embattled beltway veteran who had fought in a protracted war with no exit strategy.

The president led by the power of words. His oratory, both private and public, had a symphonic structure to it, functioning, as Sorkin describes, like "solos." From informally addressing colleagues at his chili party on the best of ourselves ("The Crackpots and These Women," 1:5) to taking on conservative radio host Dr. Jenna Jacobs (Claire Yarlett) with Bible quotations ("The Midterms," 2:3) and trouncing Governor Robert Ritchie (James Brolin) in the presidential debate ("Game On," 4:6), the Bartlet "solo" reached out and moved the listeners (and viewers) with its moral persuasion. The "solo" often seized the argument (Dr. Jacobs's anti-homosexuality stance, Rob Ritchie's call for tax cuts) to participate in a continuing oratorical dialogue about American democratic values and egalitarian ideals. In response to Ritchie's complaint about sectarian bickering, for example, Bartlet draws inspiration from the Constitution as a guide when he says that partisan politics is what the Founding Fathers "had in mind" to guarantee that minority opinions get heard. It was not only in what Bartlet said but also in the way he expressed ideas that mattered most.

Humor was often used to defuse conflict and even deflate the hubris of power. Intentional or not, self-deprecating or not, characters specialized in smart quips, witty remarks, or droll mockery. Humor translated unappealing traits—Josh's arrogance, Toby's self-righteousness, the president's know-it-all-ness—into mild eccentricity and endearing foibles. For example, in "The Drop-In," Josh wades into a debate between Bartlet and Leo on the merits of a nuclear missile defense system.

> Josh: You know. Can I just say this? Why don't we just give the $60 billion to North Korea in exchange for not bombing us?
> Bartlet: It's almost hard to believe that you're not on the National Security Council.
> Josh: I know. I feel that they're missing an important voice.

45

Comedic interruption spontaneously disrupted serious political intent, literally lightening the narrative mood. Despite feeling like comic improvisation, these carefully scripted moments of humor showcased performance skill (comic timing, verbal dexterity) but also finessed a potential narrative problem in which characters could be seen as too serious or too sanctimonious (a charge increasingly levied at the show in the post-Sorkin era). Humor also enabled characters to temporarily discard the dignified veneer of high office and, moreover, it allowed for individual relations to deepen and strengthen, often with poignancy—comic pairings, for example, included Bartlet and Leo, Toby and Sam.

It is not too surprising, then, that among other things, *The West Wing* became known for its stellar cast: from series principals to guests like Lily Tomlin, Matthew Perry, Oliver Platt, Ron Silver, Mark Harmon, and Mary-Louise Parker, and later Patricia Richardson, Stephen Root, and Janeane Garofalo. Performances met with reward—not only critical admiration and popular acclaim but industry accolades: Alan Alda (1), Janney (4), Spencer (1), Stockard Channing (1), Schiff (1), and Whitford (1) won Emmys, Sheen collected the Golden Globe for Best Actor in a TV Series Drama in 2001, Janney secured two Screen Actors Guild Awards, and the regulars received countless nominations over consecutive years.

The Politics of Decency: Screwball Dramedy

Alessandra Stanley believed that *The West Wing* might have broken "many conventions when it began . . . but one of the most startling was . . . chastity. . . . It was the most romantic show on television" (2003a, E1). Stanley was not alone. Several commentators observed how the series' simmering sexual tensions entwined with the political and were played out in the crackling dialogue, which resembled that of screwball comedies (ibid.; Holston 2003, B2; Ringelberg 2005). Attie said, "We used to joke that the Aaron seasons were the best TV shows of 1953. Which we didn't mean as a put-down; he wrote in the tradition of those great 1930s and 1940s comedies" (2010). Resuscitating such a uniquely American comedic tradition betrays a taste and cultural preference deeply embedded in the modern U.S. popular imagination (see Cavell 1981). It is a style of performing dialogue that has, as theater critic Mimi Kramer writes, "begun to seem like a cultural reference, an evocation of something innately wonderful and quintessentially American. This was our voice, our improvisation impulse" (1999).

Stanley observes that "Like the dialogue on screwball comedies written under the decency restrictions of the Hays Code, language on *The West Wing* took the place of lovemaking" (2003a, E1). Just as screwball comedies established self-imposed rules to avoid charges of indecency, the conventions

brought to network television share a similar censorial impulse, allowing the series to navigate broadcast restrictions and FCC regulations. Of course sex was implied—in the "Pilot," for example, Sam wakes up in Laurie's apartment after evidently consummating their chance encounter from the night before. But more often than not the vigor and vitality generated by intense sexual attraction were sublimated into political dispute and displays of verbal bravura.

This is perhaps contentious, but it could be argued that *The West Wing* was a screwball dramedy. Wisecracking couples clashed over ideological differences, choosing public duty over private passions, oppositions intensified by how Sorkin had absorbed the entire tradition of high-speed counterpointed dialogue since it first appeared in the screwball comedies of the 1930s before spreading into film drama and later television. Courtship rituals were, without fail, politicized, the personal *always* political. The show built on what Wes Gehring (1983) says about the screwball antihero being so absorbed in work that nothing else matters. Amy Gardner (Mary-Louise Parker) said it best when she observed, "[The White House] isn't conducive to relationships" ("Constituency of One," 5:5). Despite the obvious sexual chemistry between them, she and Josh are never able to get beyond the politics. Even while out celebrating Abbey's birthday, Amy works her angles and outmaneuvers her politically seasoned paramour ("Dead Irish Writers," 3:16).

> Josh: You went over my head and you did it behind my back.
> Amy: Quite the contortionist am I.

Innuendo aside is how wit delineates courtship. No longer can falling in love liberate a character from a deeply held political commitment to a legislative agenda. Josh and Amy split after marriage incentives are attached to the $1 billion child welfare bill, reversing an entire policy initiative on which she had campaigned ("Posse Comitatus," 3:22).

Other couples fare little better. Sam never gets beyond debating school vouchers with Mallory O'Brian (Allison Smith), an elementary school teacher and Leo's only daughter. "I despise you and everything you stand for," she declares—even

Josh and Amy take to the dance floor

though they both actually hold the same position on the issue ("Six Meetings before Lunch," 1:18). Political animosity also scuppers any chance Sam may have with Ainsley, a Republican lawyer and associate White House counsel. From the president's $1.5 billion education package ("In This White House," 2:4) to fraud prevention for small businesses ("The Lame Duck Congress," 2:6) and the Equal Rights Amendment ("17 People," 2:18), their countless political differences make it impossible for this couple to forge a lasting relationship.

Even ex-partners Toby and congresswoman Andrea "Andy" Wyatt (Kathleen York) cannot agree. Reminiscent of the divorced couple from the comedies of remarriage (1934–41), Toby and Andy are what Stanley Cavell defines as a "sophisticated pair who speak intelligently and who infuriate and appreciate one another more than anyone else" (1981, 18). They argue over mandatory minimums ("Mandatory Minimums," 1:20) and fight over language in an upcoming presidential speech on foreign policy and Islamic fundamentalism ("Night Five," 3:14). Andy eventually conceives twins through IVF with sperm collected from a time when they were married. Toby tries to win her back, weaving a policy question into a proposal of remarriage ("Debate Camp," 4:5; "Game On," 4:6). He buys her the house she has always wanted, but Andy is having none of it. "You are just too sad for me," she later says ("Commencement," 4:22). Despite being equally matched, nothing will ever change between them: the banter ultimately goes nowhere and reconciliation never leads to remarriage. They bicker about her visit to Gaza ("The Supremes," 5:17) and quarrel over Toby's protection of his source on the shuttle leak, which affects her congressional race ("Welcome to Wherever You Are," 7:15). Regardless of her fury, though, Andy respects his political integrity (as well as understands the sheer pigheadedness that comes with it) and in the penultimate episode visits C. J. to ask her help in securing a presidential pardon for Toby ("Institutional Memory," 7:21). Andy and Toby remain "forever stuck in an orbit around the foci of desire and contempt" (Cavell 1981, 19), but the romantic enterprise of that "orbit" is primarily defined by an unwavering commitment to their politics.

The political air also remains highly charged between C. J. and *Post* correspondent Danny Concannon (Timothy Busfield). The fast pace and comedic timing of their physical movements, along with sexually charged verbal exchanges, serve as a potent courting ritual. Danny persists: C. J. refuses his advances. He gives her a goldfish. They kiss—but not for long. Professional duty and personal trust become compromised when Danny writes about the contents of a strategy memo on how to beat the Bartlet team ("Let Bartlet Be Bartlet," 1:19). C. J. begs him not to run it. But it is news—and she knows it. Not quite able to slug her leading man to the floor as screwball heroines like Katharine Hepburn, Rosalind Russell, and Carole Lombard once did, C. J. finds her own way of delivering the knockout punch as she makes it difficult for him to source his stories ("Mandatory Minimums," 1:20). Such antics draw attention to both the sexual and companionable aspects of this fledgling romance. But like others before it, this relationship (temporarily) goes nowhere. As Bartlet says, he's a great reporter and she's a great press secretary and it isn't going to work while they have those jobs ("The Lame Duck Congress," 2:6). In the final season, Danny returns to Washington and asks her to "take a leap of faith" with him ("Internal Displacement," 7:11). Toby may be right when he says that working so long with "powerful and demanding men" meant that she didn't have to date, and Danny may tell her that he "doesn't want Doris Day" (the chic career woman tamed by love). But in true screwball tradition, love, marriage, and family *only* become possible for C. J. once she lets go of her professional role and starts working on her relationship with Danny away from the White House ("The Ticket," 7:1; "Institutional Memory," 7:21).

No other pairing in the show better illustrated the archetypical screwball couple than Josh and Donnatella Moss. For

C. J. and Danny as the screwball couple

five seasons it was an unequal relationship. As smart as she was loyal, Donna dutifully fetched coffee, prepared briefing memos, organized his diary, and often carried out some unenviable tasks—although she did get to hear Yo-Yo Ma ("Noël," 2:10). Perhaps more than any other, this couple represented binary opposites—and their final pairing stood for the ideal complementariness of the male-female *West Wing* relationship. Political debate exacerbated sexual tensions: a clash between intellect and emotion, reason and feeling, loyalty and attraction. In any given episode Josh and Donna battled over a range of issues— from the budget surplus ("Mr. Willis of Ohio," 1:6) to campaign finance ("Let Bartlet Be Bartlet," 1:19), from drug policy ("Ellie," 2:15) to the Mexican economy ("Bad Moon Rising," 2:19). So familiar were they with one another that they could easily pick up the threads of any given topic, which provided humor but also continually sketched their mutual compatibility. Donna acted as the "chorus" to a major political player, "the Everyperson who was the audience's access to otherwise intimidating material," says Bradley Whitford, who describes that

> part of what was fun about the relationship was kind of an Archie-Edith [Bunker] thing. Archie always thought he was the smartest guy and was always trumped by Edith, who was the wise one. In our relationship, I was always the hotshot Washington kid who needed a lot of ego to function, and people assumed I was in charge—when the truth was I couldn't have done anything without [Donna]. (quoted in Riley 2006, 30)

In Season Five, Donna had inevitably outgrown her role—and, in narrative terms, the pairing required a jolt. She asks Josh for more responsibility, and he arranges for her to join the congressional fact-finding mission to Gaza, where she falls for British photojournalist Colin Ayres (Jason Isaacs) ("Gaza," 5:21). Love blooms in the killing fields of Gaza, but tensions are never far away. Donna is seriously injured when a roadside bomb destroys the delegation vehicle in which she is traveling. Josh rushes to her bedside in a German-based military hospital, but on her return to work nothing is the same. Donna insists they talk about her future, but Josh puts off the conversation for so long that she gives up and quits ("Impact Winter," 6:9).

Donna joins Will on the Russell campaign, while Josh leads the Santos team. She starts to flourish, demonstrating flair for political strategy and media management—despite an early misstep involving an altercation with a man dressed in a chicken suit caught on camera ("Freedonia," 6:15). Working for opposing camps conspires to keep them apart. In Season Seven, after Russell exits the race, Donna approaches Josh for a job ("The Ticket," 7:1). He refuses. She hit Santos pretty hard while working for Russell, but in truth he is mad because she left him. Disloyalty, a breach of trust—it seems as if the estrangement is permanent until Lou Thornton (Janeane Garofalo), communications director for Santos's presidential campaign, recruits Donna and tells the couple to work it out ("The Al Smith Dinner," 7:6). Donna proves enterprising and politically shrewd, an equal to Josh.

After seven seasons of trials and tribulations—two near-death experiences, numerous wrong partners, and several bad dates with others—the right couple finally gets together. Like screwball couples from the 1930s, feelings only blossom into something more substantial after they share adventure traveling across America. Only when the journey ends, and there is nothing else to do but wait for election results, do Donna and Josh consummate the attraction ("Election Day Part 1," 7:16). Nothing is ever so simple, though. Josh immediately plunges himself into the maelstrom of transition before Donna gives him an ultimatum, knowing exactly how he operates with women. In the end, Donna becomes chief of staff to First Lady Helen Santos (Teri Polo) and Josh chief of staff to Santos. Each knows the political price of power but they nonetheless decide to take a chance on love anyway in keeping with the hopefulness of the series.

The Plot Thickens: Storytelling in the Age of John Wells

Alessandra Stanley wrote at the start of Season Six: "Everything is a crisis. . . . It is a little like *ER* on the Potomac—and sometimes a lot." Gone was the "banter, muttered at screwball-comedy speed and dotted with eclectic references, from St. Augustine to Gilbert and Sullivan," replaced instead with political crisis and "interpersonal melodramas" (2004). Once adoring, the interpretative community sensed that the show under Wells had become like his other series, driven too much by crisis, with "filibusters replacing defibrillators" (Holston 2005, C16). The kidnapping of Zoey marked a significant turning point. The denouement was Sorkin's last creative act before bowing out; but it also fundamentally changed the tone of the show and how the characters saw the world. Of the regime change, Richard Schiff said: "I think Aaron Sorkin is a wonderful writer in a certain style of kind of a romantic lyricism. . . . But time was running out on that kind of romantic honeymoon. . . . It's more naturalism and reality-driven drama now" (quoted in Holston 2004). Politics and family collided, and as Schiff describes, "we're now into the inner workings of a White House that was pulled apart at the seams and is struggling to hold itself together" (quoted in Holston 2005, C16).

Season Six found *The West Wing* undergoing "a makeover courtesy of the U.S. Constitution" (Goodale 2005). President Bartlet was coming to the end of his tenure, and the race to succeed him began with the show introducing Texan congressman Matthew Santos and the veteran senator Arnold Vinick from California. The focus shifted to the election cycle, culminating in the dramatic, tension-filled Democratic National Convention with Santos taking the nomination after the fourth ballot ("2162 Votes," 7:22). Each week a different civics lesson was offered on topics such as national education policy ("Opposition Research," 6:11), ethanol as an alternative fuel ("King Corn," 6:13), education, health care, and tax cuts—live ("The Debate," 7:7)—immigration and homeland security ("Message of the Week," 7:3), and nuclear power and the conflict over oil ("Duck and Cover," 7:12; "Two Weeks Out," 7:14). Of this return to debating, Wells said: "What we try to do is present the issues which our leaders are having to deal with, and show both sides of them. You try to show both sides so that the arguments are compelling and the points of view are not ridiculed" (quoted in Goodale 2005). Never before had network television fiction tackled the campaign trail in quite the way *The West Wing* did. It certainly set new stories in motion and introduced new characters—for the Santos team, Louise "Lou" Thornton, Ronna Beckman (Karis Campbell), Bram Howard (Matthew Del Negro), and Edie Ortega (Diana-Maria Riva), and for the Vinick team, Sheila Brooks (Patricia Richardson), Bob Mayer (Stephen Root), and later Jean Braun (Melinda McGraw). "This is Wells' game plan. It's similar to what he has done on *ER*—swap in a new cast for an old one to keep the show alive and cut the budget" (Murphy 2004, 9).

"No matter how talented your actors, if people are doing exactly the same jobs with the same relationships to each other, you begin to exhaust the ways in which you can get them into conflict," Wells has said. "The only thing you can really do with that is to shake it up" (quoted in Steinberg 2005, 7). Ensemble dramas with large casts always have a chance to renew and reinvent themselves in this way. Leo collapsed of a massive heart attack at Camp David after being fired by the president and the reshuffle began ("The Birnam Wood," 6:2). New jobs, fresh conflicts, and different challenges were introduced. C. J. was promoted to chief of staff, leaving a vacancy filled by Annabeth Schott (Kristin Chenoweth). Deputy national security advisor Commander Kate Harper (Mary McCormack) became a more vocal presence in the Oval Office, her advice on Israel and Palestine overriding Leo's and an ability to speak Mandarin assuring her place at the Chinese summit ("In the Room," 6:8; "Impact Winter," 6:9). Josh, Donna, and Will left for the campaign trail, the latter returning with a promotion after Toby is dismissed for leaking information about a secret military shuttle. Leo found a new role as the vice-presidential candidate on the Santos ticket; and a rather delightful working relationship developed between him and Annabeth, as she acts as his media consultant ("Mr. Frost," 7:4).

President Bartlet's physical health deteriorated ("In the Room," 6:8), but the creative jolt came not from this storyline but real life when John Spencer unexpectedly died from a heart attack at age fifty-eight on 16 December 2005. His death shocked cast and crew, to say nothing of the greater narrative dilemma of how to deal with the loss of the Democratic running mate halfway through the campaign. U.S. series have long had to deal with the death of key players—*The Sopranos* reshuffled the familial conflicts after Nancy Marchand succumbed to emphysema and lung cancer, while *Law & Order: Trial by Jury* (NBC, 2005–6) was canceled a year after the loss of Jerry Orbach. Spencer recorded what became his final episode in October and it centered on preparations for his vice-presidential debate with Governor Ray Sullivan (Brett Cullen) ("Running Mates," 7:10). The episode aired on Sunday 8 January with an introduction from Martin Sheen. It turned into a poignant tribute to the actor, but Spencer's untimely death nevertheless drastically reversed the long-term narrative fortunes of the show.

Season Seven had begun three years into the future ("The Ticket," 7:1). The Bartlet presidential library officially opens, and several of the team reunites. C. J. and Danny are now married with a daughter, living in Santa Monica; Toby lectures at Columbia University; Kate has written a book; and Will is a congressman, recently appointed to Ways and Means. Josh arrives. Obviously still working in politics, he announces, "The president is here." Before the audience gets to find out his identity the credits roll. Several of these narrative threads are worked back in the final season—C. J. heads out to California to join Danny and manage a $10 billion philanthropic foundation, Will decides to run for the difficult congressional seat in the Oregon 4th, and Toby gets a presidential pardon ("Institutional Memory," 7:21; "Tomorrow," 7:22). Given the symmetry, it might seem that a coherent narrative had long been sketched out.

Not so. Originally the writers planned for Vinick to win and take the series into its eighth year, especially since the Twenty-Second Amendment decrees it impossible for the show to continue with Bartlet. Spencer's death changed everything. Scripts had to be rewritten, and, according to Andrew Johnston, "a decision was reached to build to a natural conclusion instead of setting the stage for a new incarnation of the show" (2006). There was a sense that a Vinick victory "would prove too lopsided, in terms of taxing viewers' emotions, so a script with the new bittersweet ending—including the election night death of [Leo]—was undertaken by Wells" (Steinberg 2006, E1). A long break for the Winter Olympics afforded writers time to consider how best to resolve character arcs, and the long good-bye ended with President-Elect Santos sworn in—and President Bartlet flying home to New Hampshire.

It has long been known that the model for producing an American network TV series is about rationalizing costs. It involves creating a formula that works but also one capable of being somehow renewed. Value essentially rests with the writing and performances, for this is what keeps audiences returning week in, week out. The level of intelligence and sophisticated wit that Sorkin brought to primetime television was certainly enough to distinguish *The West Wing* as something special. Received opinion among media commentators was that once he left the show the quality of writing dipped and never recovered. Undeniably there were changes. The series emphasized plot and focused less on characters, the melodrama quotient unquestionably soared and dialogue became less nimble. Nonetheless *The West Wing* did recover its creative footing. Once it got back to its roots, exploring the politics of politics while still showing government as an honorable, even noble, pursuit, the series returned to what it did best. Scripts spoke to the higher ideals of the American creed and, at a time when a Republican with few answers occupied the real-life White House, the tone of its language and highly principled politicians with layers and subtlety came across as refreshingly defiant.

Chapter 3

Politics of the Televisual Form

Aesthetics and Sounds of Power

When Aaron Sorkin quit *The West Wing* in 2003 so did the man responsible for the distinctive look and visual style of the series, Thomas Schlamme. Sorkin wrote of him:

> [In the "Pilot" Schlamme] just mapped out what would be the first big camera move of the series, the shot that would take us inside the West Wing of the White House. We started on the bronze Seal of the President that's embedded in the floor and flowed effortlessly through the Northwest Lobby and past security and down corridors and into offices and out of offices and we got teased by the biggest office of them all before settling in and the whole thing was gonna last five minutes but seems like five seconds and it would stamp a visual style that the show would adhere to forever. *Tommy hadn't just directed the pilot, he'd just written the series in directors' language.* (2003a, 8; emphasis added)

Schlamme collected the Emmy for Outstanding Direction for this episode. It was one of five technical prizes awarded to *The West Wing* that night in September 2000. Others included

Thomas Del Ruth for Outstanding Cinematography for a Single Camera Series, and Jon Hutman (production designer), Tony Fanning (art director), and Ellen Totleben (set decorator) won for Outstanding Art Direction for a Single Camera Series for the pilot episode. Whereas television has long depended on simple shot-reverse-shot talking heads as the basis for its storytelling, the aesthetic choices made on *The West Wing* not only distinguished its distinct televisual style from that of the competition on network and cable but also gave an idealistic, ambient, and kinetic energy to a scripted political drama dealing with weighty issues and the principles and idealism behind them.

"In this show you have to *listen* to hear everything. You also have to *look* to see everything," says Schlamme (quoted in Oppenheimer 2000, 74). Prolonged Steadicam shots were a key formal element of *The West Wing,* as were the chiaroscuro shafts of contrasting light and shadow. These aesthetic principles heightened the sense of drama as characters spoke briskly while striding through the labyrinthine halls of political power. This "walk-and-talk" (also referred to as "peda-conference") established the visual signature of the show. Its use, along with a carefully crafted romantic visual quality, later becoming much darker, more sepia in tone, created a mise-en-scène of what presidential power looked and "felt" like. Yet given its privileged institutional position, *The West Wing* did not so much break with tradition as become a showcase for state-of-the-art image-making technologies and technical aestheticism that best represented the finest in U.S. television creativity. As Michael Mayers, the show's director of photography from 2004 to 2006, put it: "We work under the same production standards as the best Hollywood features" (2005). Nothing could be more tightly structured, more diligently planned and budgeted for, than *The West Wing*—but the quality of the production relied on the most up-to-date studio resources and latest technical equipment, as well as the most highly skilled creative personnel and technical operators working in American television at that time.

Like other U.S. network shows, *The West Wing* was essentially an interior piece. Filming took place on the Warner Bros. lot, and its permanently built set, covering twenty-five thousand square feet, was the biggest ever constructed for a pilot. Of this substantial investment, John Wells said: "This is the most expensive show I've ever been involved in. . . . There is a pomp and opulence surrounding our presidency which is expensive" (quoted in Waxman 2001, B3). With other parts of the set salvaged from presidential movies *Nixon* (Oliver Stone, 1995) and *The American President*, initial investment may have been high, but studio-based dramas streamline costs and rationalize production.

Library pictures of the actual 1600 Pennsylvania Avenue were extensively used as iconic establishing shots, with a second unit dispatched to Washington, D.C., to film additional location scenes of Capitol Hill and beside the Tidal Basin of the Potomac—recognizable sights of the nation's capital. Schlamme talked of the production team making "three or four trips" a year to the city and banking "three or four scenes from different episodes" (quoted in Abramson 2007, 218). Location filming helped punctuate the important White House corridors and offices where most scenes were shot, contributing a pace and "feel" for the city where the political drama unfolded. These shots physically mapped out the limited ten-square-mile world in which dedicated staffers operated (and made the disorientation of Josh and Toby lost in the middle of America with only Donna to guide them back inside the beltway even funnier ["20 Hours in America," 4:1, 4:2]). But the repeated images of the White House—a symbol of the presidency, American government, and its people—served as a constant reminder of the democratic importance of what these characters did—and why they so rarely left the office.

Filming may have included interiors with sets and props designed for verisimilitude, but how "the building" was laid out mapped the series' political mind-set. Implanted right into its production design and highly refined aesthetic choices was the idea of watching the democratic political process at work. From the grandeur of the Northwest Lobby (reconstructed to look as it did during the JFK presidency) to the semi-open-planned space of the bullpen (where too many people are crowded into too few places), from the Roosevelt Room (with its French doors revealing the incessant process of governance) to the Oval Office (the inner sanctum where power is conducted in the round), the space visualized the constitutionally determined republican character of participatory politics where the people's representatives assemble and speak to executive power—or, as Toby remarks, "a place where people come together and where no one gets left behind" ("He Shall, From Time to Time . . . ," 1:12). Everything was important; no opinion went unheard along the corridors and in the offices of this White House. Debating ideas and respecting pluralism, as the hour rolled by, staged for theatrical purposes the spectacle of what American democracy should look and "feel" like.

The Politics of Steadicam: Space, Performance, and Democracy

A Steadicam moving with speed and efficiency through the labyrinthine but interconnecting walkways further served to stage the drama, inviting a medley of opinions and encounters, policy ideas and political crises. The Steadicam—a camera rigged with a counterweight that enables the operator to move while it remains absolutely steady—has long been a feature of film production. But time constraints and exorbitant costs prohibited its crossover into television until 1994, when Del Ruth pioneered its use in *ER*, which, as Jean Oppenheimer claims, "changed the way people thought about staging and shooting a weekly program" (2000, 74). Perhaps more than any other cinematographer, Del Ruth used the Steadicam in the most innovative ways, allowing for a particular dramatic pace and rhythm. Of *The West Wing*, Del Ruth acknowledged that "the most difficult thing was coming up with the original concept for how the White House should look, and then plotting out all the instruments that would be needed . . . that would not only be efficient to work with, but also dramatically appropriate" (quoted in ibid., 75).

In adopting lengthy Steadicam tracking shots, the "walk-and-talk" enabled the series to visually compensate for what it relinquished to commercial rivals, such as HBO, or feature film production with extensive on-location shoots. Aided by a complex lighting design system (including "bat lights," which provide long, narrow strips of illumination, and Kino Flos wrapped in gels hidden in columns), the Steadicam shot invigorated the field of vision, imbuing it with an astonishing dramatic vigor and spatial depth. Filming an actor walking through such a space, striding beneath strong pools of downlighting with its resulting strobe effect, "gave an accentuated sense of motion" (Del Ruth quoted in ibid., 83), a sense of this world being full of polemic opinions and difficult decisions.

Whereas most series give over a complete scene to a single topic, *The West Wing* had so much business to get through that it chose instead "to break single scenes into separate dramatic mini-scenes . . . unrelated to each other narratively but which shared the same time and space" (Smith 2003, 128). Only with the Steadicam could the dramatic potential of staging political debate be truly realized. It gave coherence to the shards of dialogue and conversational fragments; it provided "a visual unity that counterbalanced the verbally fractured snippets, making it possible for the show to make longer eloquent statements" (ibid., 131).

Creating aesthetic cohesion from the highly polished sound bites, snatched conversations, and characters only momentarily taking center stage before being replaced by others made visible a democratic discourse and deliberation—albeit from a leftish perspective. The "longer eloquent statements" engaged the citizen-audience, inspiring civics lessons and drawing citizens enthusiastically into the realm of the political, often showing realities that are obscured from view. In that regard, the aesthetic and technical choices defining what the politics looked like proved a way through which the citizen-audience could make sense of how power worked.

One of the longest and most complicated Steadicam shoots occurs in "Five Votes Down" (1:4); it lasted nearly three minutes and was filmed at the Ambassador Hotel in Los Angeles. It starts with Bartlet delivering a speech on the gun control bill at a black-tie event for Democrats. Behind him a banner reads "Practical Idealism." He rallies the audience (and viewers) to get involved, to be part of the process. The president talks of the law, of the facts being on their side. Immediately the scene alerts us to what Alexis de Tocqueville already had observed about American democracy in 1840: that intellectual life was distinguished by a practical concern for solving the difficulties of the everyday. As the president ratchets up the rhetoric in the full glare of the media spotlight, senior staffers work backstage, toiling in the shadows, on the prosaic business of turning eloquence into law. Leo and Josh learn that they have lost five votes on the Hill and start to make their calls, while Toby intently listens to Bartlet's delivery, which builds to its crescendo: "We're going to win on Wednesday." The crowd rises to its feet and the band starts playing "Happy Days Are Here Again." Bartlet comes off the stage, out of the spotlight, and into the wings of political power.

So begins the classic "walk-and-talk." Along with the principals, five hundred extras were involved, and it was completed in one seamless Steadicam shot, of which Del Ruth said: "It was about a five page scene and took us half the night [to shoot]. Dave [Chameides, the Steadicam operator] was walking backward at full speed for the entire shot; on take 13, he almost collapsed!" (quoted in Oppenheimer 2000, 80–81). Over the next few minutes the show's central characters come and go, delivering policy news and exchanging gossip, joking with each other and offering advice.

Bartlet walks off the stage and into the lobby. Sam congratulates him. No sooner has Bartlet thanked him then he moves out of shot followed by his security detail. Toby moves in and Sam falls in next to him, with the rest of the team in pairs not far behind. They strike up a conversation about the speech, and the camera picks up their pace as staffers briskly march down the hallway. "Good job," Sam enthuses. Toby is brooding: "It was fine." "It was outstanding," responds Sam. "He blew the D-Section," replies Toby. C. J. chimes in, congratulating Sam. "Tell him," he replies. Why? "'Cause he wrote two-and-a-half paragraphs and I wrote thirty-seven pages," says Toby, his vexation over the "D-section" evident in the rising cadence of his voice. The camera trails behind the principals as they descend a flight of stairs. Josh appears beside C. J. She switches topics, commenting on the presence of Josh's "little fan club." Without missing a beat, C. J. asks Josh if he thinks she has "an unusually large neck." Josh is nonplussed by the non sequitur. C. J. is bothered that she may appear risible. "Stop talking," he tells her. He wants her to stay calm, informing her that they have lost five votes on 802 (the gun-control bill on which Bartlet has just spoken). As they reach the kitchens the camera draws level with the couple and C. J. remains anything but calm. She wants names. On the beat of Leo shouting, "Josh!" the camera focuses on a secret service man talking into his walkie-talkie as he moves between Sam and Mandy, whose conversation now takes center stage. Sam questions the wisdom of the musical choice "Happy Days Are Here Again" after the president has just spoken about kids being gunned down. As they debate the decision, the camera moves ahead and Toby comes back into shot. With the chat concluded, another secret service agent appears to block Sam and Mandy off, leaving the president room to re-enter the scene and walk beside Toby as they descend another flight of stairs into the hotel catacombs.

Bartlet asks his communications director what he thought of the delivery. Toby cannot help but ask about what happened in the D-section. Bartlet confesses that he gave it a little polish, right up there on his feet, although he half-feared Toby would come at him with a salad fork. But for the secret service agents restraining him comes the sardonic reply. Catching sight of a canoodling couple, Bartlet breaks off to casually joke that the guy should buy the woman some supper. Toby laughs. No sooner has Charlie caught up with the president then he, too, is drawn into the discussion about the text of the speech versus its delivery. Given the length of the scene, that sense of how Toby *lives* his writing, of how he cannot help but articulate every last thought, can be represented in full. Toby is never funnier than when he is living the pain and anxiety of how his text has been delivered—or not.

Yet the exchange abruptly ends with Bartlet asking if the First Lady called, giving Charlie a chance to ask if the president has taken his back medicine. As the party exits the building, the assembled crowds cheer, the lights of the security vehicles flash, and Charlie impresses on the president that his wife's tone was most insistent. "You don't have to describe the tone to me. I've been married to it for thirty-two years." Bartlet promises to take the "damn" medicine, bids Charlie goodnight, and waves to the crowd before climbing into the back of a limousine. At this point the camera moves back and onto three members of Josh's fan club shouting, "We love you, Josh," as the deputy chief of staff passes by with C. J. in tow. "Thanks," he says, nonchalantly waving back. C. J. swings around. "It helps not to know him." The scene concludes with Josh and C. J. exchanging gestures. Cut to credits.

This continuous take, which lasted two minutes and fifty-two seconds, coheres the idle chat, light banter, gentle mocking, and heated political exchanges; it gives the fast-paced, almost breathless verbal delivery a visceral energy akin to theater or live television. "As an actor, I adore walk-and-talk because I spent the first 20 years of my career onstage, and it's the closest to stage work in that there's no intercutting," said John Spencer (quoted in Ruditis and Jackman 2002, 26). Like him, many of the ensemble cast—Hill, Janney, Schiff, Whitford—trained and worked in the theater; and to a large degree, Steadicam technology replicates those staging conditions, demanding that the actor execute continuous long takes while demonstrating, as casting director John Frank Levey puts it, "a skill with language . . . much greater than most television scripts require" (quoted in Kuhn 2006, 28).

Within a matter of moments Whitford communicates sharp political intelligence (how to negotiate lost votes), hubris in his swagger (retribution *will* be sought for defectors), and an awkward boyish charm (related to his "little fan club"). Janney demonstrates elegance in her poise with her elongated six-foot frame and long expressive arms. She performs stylish wit like a throwback to Rosalind Russell in *His Girl Friday* (goading Toby); she is sassy (poking fun at Josh's fan club) but vulnerable beneath the self-confidence (not liking what her long neck implies about her). Her facial expressions register emotional subtleties, breaking into raucous laughter as she teases Toby, before darkening with wide-eyed incredulity at the news that they are five votes down. "Nice job at looking calm," says Josh. The Steadicam makes all of this possible because it allows the actors to exhibit a repertoire of performance skills in one continuous take. Because the Steadicam is able to follow the action and film without edited interruptions, "everyone has to hit their marks and be at the top of their game" (Mayers 2005). Put simply, the actor can perform like this *only* because the camera technology privileges this way of working.

Patrick Finn asserts that in *The West Wing* the Steadicam's "equalizing technology . . . reaches out to the viewing pub-

C. J. jokes with Sam and Toby

C. J. doesn't take the news well.

lic and says everything is okay. The office may be moving fast, and the political issues may be complicated, but you are stable" (2003, 116). It is a provocative claim, but the Steadicam also evokes what André Bazin (1972) referred to as the "phenomenological integrity" embedded in image-making technology: a filmmaker should not interfere with reality but instead replicate or reproduce as authentic a reality as possible by allowing the camera to simply watch. Reliance on protracted Steadicam tracking shots gives the audience not only a different perspective of space but also an alternative conception of it. The Steadicam draws the viewer into the narrative action in ways that more conventional camerawork and editing fail to do. It allows for a different, more direct approach to staging the drama, as well as a reconceptualization of the political sphere. This image-making technology in *The West Wing* offered unprecedented access to politics behind the headlines—and there was a constant interplay between multiple televisions tuned to the different news channels, full of sound bites, spin, and spectacle, and the implied transparency and democracy of textual address promised by the Steadicam as it moves effortlessly between private spaces and the public sphere.

Aesthetics of Power

"I always felt this show was a presentation of an optimistic White House, a Camelot for the masses," reflects Del Ruth (quoted in Oppenheimer 2000, 74). Of course, as Melissa Crawley points out, the Camelot metaphor carries associations of the Kennedy White House and the fabled court of King Arthur. It creates, she argues, "a mythic vision of a presidency experienced through layers of fiction and fact" (2006, 111). Moreover, this vision of the presidency is about creating myths of American presidential power—duty and loyalty, honorable individuals fighting for higher principles, and a magical beauty—and how those ideas inscribed right into the aesthetic choices and forms as the series inherited and used them.

The West Wing began with a decidedly hopeful vision. "To help sell that idea," Del Ruth says, "we wanted a softer, veiled image that had a golden quality, as well as strong backlighting and contrast" (quoted in Oppenheimer 2000, 74). Almost as pervasive as the Steadicam was the Technocrane, which allowed for a broader sweep depicting the elevating oratory and grandeur of the presidential office. Choices of apricot, rose, and russet-colored Rosco gels, along with the somber hues of blues and greens of the Mural Room, dominated the color palette; diffused lighting smoothed out harsh edges; and icons of American history—portraits of George Washington, Abraham Lincoln, and Theodore Roosevelt, as well as scenes from the Revolutionary War, or American War of Independence (1775–83), in the Mural Room—adorn the walls. This was a White House that visually depicted optimism and hope but at the same time historical gravitas and darker moods with its noir-ish lighting indicating the political machinations behind the scenes. This mise-en-scène of presidential power also provided a stage for the soaring rhetoric that spoke of a nation's best ideals—democratic freedom and patriotic fortitude, self-determinism and enterprise.

At the end of the "Shibboleth" episode (2:8), in which the administration deals with Chinese evangelists fleeing persecution in their native land, as well as a presidential pardon for a turkey, Bartlet meets with Josh and Sam, where the president informs his deputy chief of staff that the Latin word for yam is *dioscorea*. Josh lets it go but asks instead if he had heard that the refugees "escaped." Bartlet feigns incredulity and starts to read from the Thanksgiving Proclamation prepared by Sam. "Well over three-and-a-half centuries ago, strengthened by faith and bound by a common desire for liberty, a small band of pilgrims sought out a place in the New World where they could worship according to their own beliefs." He pauses over the power of the

Inside the Oval Office

words. Soft shadows and warm, mellow light fill the room, and children's voices are heard off camera. Josh inquires: "So the guy passed the test, huh?" (in reference to how the president intended to ascertain whether the faith of the Chinese refugee, Jhin Wei [Henry O], was feigned or not). The president spins around. The pale evening light filters through the French doors creating a soft halo effect around him.

> Bartlet: You think I would send him back if he failed catechism? Let me tell you something, we can be the world's policemen, we can be the world's bank, the world's factory, the world's farm . . . what does it mean if we're not also . . . [Pause.] They made it to the New World, Josh. [Pause.] And do you know what I get to do now? [Beat.] I get to proclaim a national day of Thanksgiving.

He smiles benevolently and the two men leave for the Rose Garden. Lute playing and children's voices raised in song, "We Gather Together," accompany the final image of Gilbert Stuart's iconic portrait of George Washington seen almost shimmering through the glass panes of the Oval Office. Soft-hued autumnal light and pastel shades—apricots, the yellowish-white color of vanilla—fill the image. This bucolic mise-en-scène conveys the Bartlet presidential mystique of a compassionate patriarch, assuring hope for America, while inseparable from its history, going right back to the Founding Fathers. (And let's not forget, it is in this episode that the president gives Charlie the knife made for the Bartlet family by a Boston silversmith named Paul Revere. It has been passed down by proud fathers ever since. "I'm proud of you, Charlie," Bartlet says.)

Over time, this romantic optimism gave way to a darker, more sober vision. Nowhere is this better illustrated than in how the mise-en-scène conveyed a certain fatalism about the direction in which Bartlet took his presidency—the nation and his family. A crucial turning point comes at the end of Season Three (airing nine months after 9/11) when Bartlet sanctions the covert political assassination of Qumari defense minister and terrorist leader Abdul Shareef (Al No'mani). Bartlet makes his fateful decision while attending a benefit performance of *The Wars of the Roses* based on William Shakespeare's history plays, in which private intrigue and petty jealousies plunged England into the dynastic civil wars of the fifteenth century ("Posse Comitatus," 3:22). The setting for Bartlet's initial meeting with Leo echoes the epic struggle being enacted onstage: motifs from the play (such as flags) decorate the baroque interior, the long, deserted gallery where secret deals are done, warm light and ominous shadows heightening the intrigue. The stage is set for the two men to conspire. Shot in tight close-up and using a shot-reverse-shot pattern, Bartlet must weigh political expediency and national security against religious ethics and moral integrity. That America joins "the league of ordinary nations" is his objection. "It's wrong. It's absolutely wrong." "I know," replies Leo, "but you have to do it anyway." The sound of silence hangs heavily over both men. "Take him," intones the president. That he does, without congressional approval, turns Bartlet into an "imperial president," a term coined by Arthur Schlesinger Jr. (2004) to describe how war expands presidential power.

The season finale climaxes with a thunderous chorus of "And victorious in war shall be made glorious in peace," cutting between the theatrical production and the covert assassination of Shareef. The cost of democracy and rise of the imperial Bartlet presidency is staged with the spotlighting of a teenage boy dashing onstage, singing "England Arise." Around him in vague darkness bodies lie fallen in the chaos of battle, but soon the stage starts to bustle with life as the chorus gathers in song. There is a cut to guns being handed out among U.S. Marines under the cover of dark. A shot of a Navy Seal looking through his night goggles at Shareef's plane landing cuts to a woman in the audience watching the performance through opera glasses. The clandestine theater of modern war on terror plays out against the celebratory pomp of the Shakespearean histories. Lighting—the stage lights, the flash of gunfire—heightens the atmospheric tension. The same is true of the cutting between covert operations in Bermuda, Admiral Percy Fitzwallace (John Amos) in the situation room waiting for news, Leo lurking in the shadows expecting Fitzwallace's call, the full chorus waving flags in the glare of the spotlight, and Bartlet in his front-row seat. The scene builds to the president swathed in gloom, his lone profile silhouetted behind a falling drape. The curtain falls—on the play, the episode, and the season. Monarchs in Shakespeare's history plays, Peter Conrad reminds us, are "judged according to the skill with which they play the king" (2000, 2). In that spirit, the mise-en-scène reminds us that the presidency, too, is about performance. But in how the sequence redefines how Bartlet will perform the presidency, the scene recalls what G. K.

Chesterton said about "The American Republic [as] the last mediaeval monarchy" and how its popular presidents "have acted as democratic despots" (1922, 122).

The consequences of his action nearly bring down the House of Bartlet. On the international stage, Qumar uses the incident to get aggressive with Israel, shooting down a plane carrying Ben Yosef (Malachi Throne), a high-ranking Israeli official and friend of Leo's ("The Red Mass," 4:4). Closer to home, a local terrorist cell abducts Zoey while she is out celebrating her graduation from Georgetown ("Commencement," 4:22), which results in Bartlet invoking the Twenty-Fifth Amendment and abdicating his role as president ("Twenty-Five," 4:23).

Gone (temporarily) was the smooth Steadicam aesthetic, replaced instead by unsettling camera work, a darker mood, and a bolder color palette. Leo is dispatched to tell Bartlet that Walken plans to bomb Qumar ("7A WF 83429," 5:1). The chief of staff steps off the elevator and walks along a long, dark corridor, with only low orbs of orange light to guide him. There is an ominous sense of doom and portent. He finds Bartlet alone in the residence, staring out of a "prison"-like window on his

Bartlet as the "Imperial President"

threatened realm. Darkness looms around him, and he casts a long shadow on the wall behind. Despite the idle chat, the mood between the men is lit by low-key lighting, with minimal fill light, and atmospheric shadows tinted by a richly textured color palette with an intense deep red molding Bartlet's weary face and electric blue shading Leo's. Its theatricality is indebted to film noir, a textual echo that reverberated across the series. Yet this time it is different. The noir-ish staging at this heightened emotional moment speaks to the darker political realities of power and gives representation to a mournful melancholia of something irretrievably lost—a beloved daughter for sure but also political purpose, a vision for America. Bartlet says, "All these things we wanted to do, Leo. All the things we believed in and wanted to fight for." Leo nods. Bartlet does not need his friend to tell him what Walken intends to do; he knows. No words are necessary. Instead, the mise-en-scène speaks to one of the show's unifying themes, the distorting pressures of political realities compromising higher principles.

As Season Five began, *The West Wing* adopted a different aesthetic tone as the presidency entered a new phase. The image became sharper with a higher resolution—no doubt related in part to the growth of HDTV, as well as increased installation of state-of-the-art home entertainment systems. The aesthetic became more sepia in tone. Just as the clock started to run out on the Bartlet presidency, the photograph was starting to fade. A harsher, more muted color palette was adopted. Gone were the softly veiled, romantic images, replaced instead with darker shades of reddish brown, slate blue, and golden yellow. These deeper, richer colors conveyed a sense of maturity, of how the office had fundamentally changed the man. Decisions started to weigh more heavily on Bartlet as he returned to work and tried to get back to running the country as he had initially envisioned. The mise-en-scène represented the highest political endeavor and gave a sense of a cause that remained noble and true despite the compromises Bartlet had to make along the way.

Michael Mayers took over from Del Ruth as director of photography for the final two seasons. With the narrative out on the campaign trail, the aesthetic became more bleached out and often referenced the techniques of Direct Cinema and cinema verité. "Opposition Research" (6:11) starts out with a blank white screen before dissolving into an establishing shot of snow-covered fields with a single car driving through an empty landscape. In the vehicle are Representative Matt Santos and Josh as they begin their journey from New Hampshire to the White House. As the campaign progresses, the filming echoed in its formal DNA a documentary style reminiscent of Direct Cinema films such as *Primary*, which followed Democrat presidential hopefuls John F. Kennedy and Hubert Humphrey during the 1960 Wisconsin primary. It was filmed by Richard Leacock and Albert Maysles with what was then state-of-the art 16-millimeter portable sync-sound equipment. Textual reverberations were there in *The West Wing*'s use of the shaky, mobile camera and the way in which this aesthetic choice re-created spontaneity and a greater intimacy. The roving camera followed directly behind the candidates as they moved through the assembled crowds, crammed with them into busy restaurants and private homes ("Opposition Research," 6:11), and lingered on their facial reactions before a stump speech ("King Corn," 6:13; "Freedonia," 6:15) or while negotiating political deals ("La Palabra," 6:18). The Direct Cinema aspiration to show how things really were also gave us access to the back-room trading and dirty tricks, as the Democratic campaign teams tried to secure the nomination for their candidate ("2162 Votes," 6:22).

As the presidential campaign gathered momentum, the pace remained fast and furious. Jerky camera movements, frantic Steadicam, and fast cutting rates became more common. In "The Mommy Problem" (7:2), Santos's whirlwind schedule is edited together with abrupt jump cuts of snapshot images as

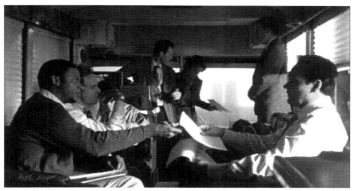

On the campaign trail with Santos

the candidate meets and greets the electorate with energy and youthful vigor. Harsh fluorescent overhead lights and almost bleached-out colors communicated the relentless pace and exhaustion of fighting a long and hotly contested campaign. "Welcome to Wherever You Are" (7:15) replicated the style of cinema verité as the Santos campaign "flies with the sun" across the country. Smash cuts and fragmented conversations disorient the viewer, and the shaky, handheld camera conveys the experience of sleep-deprived staffers having slightly lost their bearings on the relentless campaign trail.

Sounds of Power

In September 2000 W. G. Snuffy Walden walked away with an Emmy for Main Title Theme Music. Walden admits in the "Sheet Music" bonus featurette from the complete *West Wing* box-set that the intention was to break the mold of how fictional representations of the presidency were traditionally scored. Each week, following a narrative review and opening teaser, his main title score erupted onto the screen with a smash cut and crash of cymbals. A rippling curtain of the U.S. flag gives way to the seal of the president. Lush rousing orchestral strings emotionally draw the audience into the drama with a "melody that underscores the power of the presidency" (Elber 2001). Waves of orchestral and electronic sound combine into a "big sweeping expanse of music" (Lambert 2000), as colored images of the leading players at work are juxtaposed with intimate black-and-white portraits of them. Political past and presidential present, patriotism and nationhood, history as intimately experienced, are woven together into a fanfare saturated in the sounds of Americana. "It's a little bit of Taps [a musical piece sounded nightly by the U.S. military], a little bit of gospel and a little bit of [Aaron] Copland," says Walden (quoted in Elber 2001).

In the first four seasons, when the verbal, rhythmic musical patterns of the dialogue dominated, incidental music either punctuated a scene or created a "feeling" for a character. Popular songs rarely played a narrative role. One exception was the non-diegetic playing of Dire Straits/Mark Knopfler's "Brothers in Arms" (1985) to bridge the climatic moments ending Season Two ("Two Cathedrals," 2:22). It is a piece of pure television theater with Bartlet pushed to the emotional brink: Mrs. Landingham is dead and laid to rest, his MS is public, and he must decide whether to seek reelection. Events have triggered memories of times gone by, and this most eloquent of presidents (this is the episode where, with anger, arrogance, and sheer hubris, he delivers his diatribe to God in Latin) is quite literally lost for words. The season finale, with its two worlds working in parallel, functions as a memory piece, as Bartlet sifts through recollections to unlock a moment in his past that will help him decide what to do next. A howling tropical storm rages over Washington as the first bluesy, languorous chords of the song reverberate. Bartlet steps out of the Oval Office and onto the portico as the rain lashes down. He gets drenched; it is, as Sorkin says, the re-baptism of Bartlet, filling him with a renewed sense of political purpose. Thunderclaps, pouring rain, and the sound of the high winds are overlaid with the low, rumbling sounds of the song's instrumental beginning. Charlie rushes out with a coat: "It's time."

As Bartlet reenters the building, shutting out the noise of the storm, the lyrics guide his journey in silence from the Oval Office to the Commerce Department, where he will make his announcement. As he walks with resolve through the West Wing, he is joined by his loyal lieutenants—Leo, Sam and Josh, Toby, Charlie, accompanied by Knopfler's husky vocals singing of those returning from battle: "And you'll no longer burn / To be brothers in arms." At the end of the first verse, there is a cut to the bedlam of the press conference where C. J. is fielding questions, her voice barely heard over the ebb and flow of the guitar solo. During the second stanza, an additional beat is introduced as Bartlet's wordless journey continues, shifting between private spaces and the public sphere. Inside the National Cathedral an African American custodian picks up a cigarette (extinguished earlier by Bartlet in an act of defiance, perhaps desecration, against his father, mixed in his mind with God) but is distracted by the lights of the passing presidential motorcade. "There's so many different worlds / So many different suns" rings out, while there is a cut to Bartlet looking out of the limo window, almost as if to return the gaze. Just as the storm gathers pace, so does the thunderous orchestration as the president arrives at his destination—both literally and metaphorically. C. J. introduces him ("Every man has to die"), and Bartlet mounts the podium. His decision made, this is his destiny ("But it's written in the starlight / And every line on your palm"). The music lowers and then swells as the team look on in bewildered anticipation as Bartlet fails to call on the reporter C. J. has set up to ask the first question. Turning away from viewing the TV monitor, Leo says, "Watch this"—reminding viewers to stay tuned for the next season. The camera swirls around Bartlet as the guitar solo builds a sense of expectancy. He turns away, smiles, and puts his hands into his pockets. The audience knows what that body language means (even though they must wait three months to see if that interpretation is correct), explained by the young Dolores Landingham (Kirsten Nelson) in the flashbacks—it means he'll do it. The sequence ends with a fade to black.

Greg Smith notes that highly foregrounded pieces of music are used as "codas of considerable power" (2003, 134). Over and again, *The West Wing* used "a song to create a particularly lyrically coordinated finale" (ibid.). "Brothers in Arms," combined with the growling sounds of the raging tropical storm, articulates Bartlet's political reawakening. Jeff Buckley's achingly poignant interpretation of Leonard Cohen's song "Hallelujah" serenades the montage immediately following the death of secret service agent and love interest for C. J., Simon Donovan (Mark Harmon) ("Posse Comitatus," 3:22). Donovan lies slain after a random act of violence, and Buckley's bittersweet rendition provides a narrative capsule for the episode to explore human frailty, unfolding grief, and palpable loss (C. J. absorbing the news), as well as the traitorousness of love (Josh politically outflanking Amy over a key welfare reform bill)—as the narrative escalates to Bartlet authorizing the clandestine execution of Shareef.

Some of the lyrics evoke Hebrew stories from the Old Testament of passions that threaten to bring down kingdoms—the adulterous affair of Bathsheba and David ("You saw her bathing on the roof / Her beauty and the moonlight overthrew you") and Delilah's betrayal of Samson ("She broke your throne and she cut your hair"). But the quiet, almost ethereal intensity Buckley brings to these lines changes the mood, and his light, lyrical vocals underline C. J.'s despair on hearing the news of Donovan's unforeseen death. The next lines ("Baby I've been here before / I've seen this room and I've walked the floor [you know]") are barely audible above the intense but measured argument between Josh and Amy. She is resigning her position after Josh cuts a deal with her boss, effectively reversing an "entire policy initiative" on which Amy had worked. Underscoring their increasingly bitter quarrel are lyrics that speak of love soured and gone stale: "And I've seen your flag on the marble arch / and love is not a victory march / It's a cold and it's a broken Hallelujah." The fragile falsetto of Buckley thus maps this passionate relationship that never seems able to get beyond the politics. The song finally dies away with its repeated chorus of "Hallelujah," as Leo, shot from a low angle, goes to meet with Bartlet, struggling with the uneasy decision to give the order to assassinate Shareef. Weaving biblical references into this melancholic hymn to love, gospel rhythms mixed with a waltz, the song sung by Buckley textually layers with intricacy and nuance the personal cost of political power.

Sometimes songs operated as the soundtrack to a particular episode. Offering subtextual commentary on the narrative, these recordings took on a decidedly political role. In "The Warfare of Genghis Khan" (5:13), Blind Willie Johnson's haunting blues/spiritual "Dark Was the Night, Cold Was the Ground" is mentioned by Josh to illustrate the sublime ambition behind the U.S. space project to "do something else, something generous, uplifting" with American "economic supremacy" and "technological dominance." (The Voyager Golden Record, sent into space on Voyager in 1977, included the song.) At the end of the episode, the haunting slide guitar combined with Johnson's raspy false-bass vocals provide the musical accompaniment to Josh's star-gazing while Bartlet remains earthbound in the situation room watching satellite images of an underwater nuclear test carried out by the Israelis in the Indian Ocean.

No other song delivers the political message more powerfully than James Taylor's acoustic version of Sam Cooke's "A Change Is Gonna Come" ("A Change Is Gonna Come," 6:7). Taylor, himself long associated with environmental and liberal causes, performed the cover version during the Season Six episode, which first aired in December 2004, at the end of an election year when Taylor joined the "Vote for Change" tour to mobilize support for Democrat nominee Senator John Kerry in the swing states. Taylor has "insisted on joining" the celebrations at the Bartlet White House, as the president awards a posthumous medal for achievement in the arts to Sam Cooke, soul music pioneer and activist in the American civil rights movement, for which "A Change Is Gonna Come" became an anthem. Diegetically motivated as part of the event, Taylor starts to sing what he calls a "classic song . . . that has echoed down the generations." His smooth, understated delivery of the lyrics' yearning for change provided a sound bridge for what happens next.

With the line "It's been a long, a long time coming" the scene shifts from the official reception to C. J. taking a call from former vice president Hoynes, followed by a cut to Josh, alone in his office, looking at Hoynes's new book, *Full Disclosure* (part personal apology for sexual indiscretions, part public statement of political principles). Josh lingers over the handwritten inscription, "JOSH, TIME TO LEAD, JOHN" as Taylor's slow, ethereal voice rings out, "I don't know what's up there beyond the sky / It's been a long, long time coming." Josh scans the index and finds thirty-nine "Lyman" references. His dawning realization as to what that means is underscored by a slight reworking of the lyrics: "But I know that change is gonna come / You know I had a talk with my brother." There is at that moment a cut to Toby at the reception, joined by C. J., where the two silently acknowledge that she *doesn't* appear in the book. (C. J. had a deeply regretted one-night stand with Hoynes many years ago.) With a line now drawn under that past, the scene shifts to Josh meeting Hoynes at night. There is another slight reworking of the lyrics—"There been times that I thought I won't last too long / Somehow I have been able to just about carry on"—as Josh gets into Hoynes's car and the former vice president confesses that despite his fall from grace he *will* seek the Democratic nomination.

Meanwhile at the reception, and accompanied by a repeat of the verses underscoring the above, Bartlet whispers to Abbey that the diplomatic furor over the Taiwanese independence flag (which consumes staffers for most of the episode) happened because he could not see out of his right eye. Back in the noir shadows Hoynes wants Josh to run his campaign. There is a cut to black, as the song finishes with, "Yes, a change is gonna come." This melancholic song, sung by Taylor with his restrained, almost introspective delivery, marks an important and poignant turning point in the longer dramatic arc. It signals a shift, as Bartlet enters the twilight of his presidency struggling with MS and striving for a legacy, while the search for his successor begins.

President-Elect Barack Obama paraphrased "A Change Is Gonna Come" in his victory speech in November 2009: "It's been a long time coming, but tonight, because of what we did on this day, in this election, at this defining moment, change has come to America." Coincidence probably, but it is a testament to the song's status in the American songbook. Using the tune as the show did, however, represents yet another moment when *The West Wing* captured a sense of the political imagination in its formal textual structure. This episode aired following President Bush's second-term victory, but in the lyrical longing for change, and sung by a performer who bridged the divide between 1960s activism and 1970s political introspection, the use of "A Change Is Gonna Come" provided a vivid soundtrack to that liberal yearning for something different—to which, for seven years, *The West Wing* gave representation.

"Modern History Is Another Name for Television"

Representing Historical Relevancy and Cultural Memory

*T*he West Wing debuted as a mildly successful show but, by the following spring, "[had] caught fire in the press, with cover stories in major magazines and articles in major newspapers" (Podhoretz 2003, 222). Writing for the now defunct political lifestyle magazine *George*, Sharon Waxman concluded that the beltway drama had "become that rarest of rarities on the pop-culture landscape: a *zeitgeist* show, a reflection of the tenor of our times" (2003, 206). This notion of the series as somehow making sense of the post–cold war and later post-9/11 world, dialoguing with the troubled Clinton administration before acting as the liberal imagination to a conservative reality under the Republican presidency of George W. Bush, defined for many scholars and media commentators the milestone significance of *The West Wing*.

Never before had a television drama about presidential politics captured the popular imagination in quite the way that *The West Wing* did. Whether real or imaginary, celluloid presidents have, by contrast, long thrived in the movies: from President William McKinley filmed by the Edison Company taking the oath of office in 1901 and Henry Fonda as Abraham Lincoln in John Ford's 1939 classic *Young Mr. Lincoln* to John Travolta as the philandering yet politically gifted Governor Jack Stanton (a thinly disguised Bill Clinton) in *Primary Colors* (Mike Nichols, 1998)—including a fine cameo performance by Allison Janney as the librarian made so nervous by Stanton that she falls *up* the stairs. Then there was Sorkin's prelude to *The West Wing, The American President,* in which Andrew Shepherd was staffed by some familiar faces: Martin Sheen as chief of staff A. J. MacInerney, Anna Deavere Smith in the role of press secretary Robin McCall, and Joshua Malina as David, an advisor—while not forgetting Nina Siemaszko as Sydney Ellen Wade's younger sibling.

On television, the presidency has more often than not been the subject of late-night satire, from *The Smothers Brothers Comedy Hour* (CBS, 1967–70) (with the fictitious "Pat Paulsen for President" campaign) to *Saturday Night Live* (NBC, 1975–present) (including Will Ferrell's impersonation of George W. Bush and Fred Armisen's Barack Obama). It is discussed on the Sunday morning talk shows and is often the theme of documentary specials. Rarely is it depicted in drama. "Quality shows about politics," observes veteran TV watcher Marvin Kitson, "have always failed, a tradition dating back to Hal Holbrook's *The Senator* [NBC, 1970–71]" (2000 B2). From *Hail to the Chief* (1985), starring Patty Duke as the first female president, to George C. Scott taking the eponymous title role in *Mr. President* (FOX, 1987–88); from *Tanner '88,* HBO's satirical series about a fictitious Democratic contender from director Robert Altman and Doonesbury creator Garry Trudeau, to Comedy Central's sardonic sitcom *That's My Bush* (2001), starring Timothy Bottoms as George W., shelved soon after 9/11. Often lasting no longer than one season, television shows about the denizens of 1600 Pennsylvania Avenue have long found it hard to find a viewing constituency.

Until, that is, *The West Wing*.

It is impossible to disregard the reverberations of the popular media in real-world politics. Only in this modern age of saturated twenty-four-hour news coverage, in fact, does *The West Wing* somehow become possible. It was during the Clinton administration that the presidency and political process became "demystified" as never before. One reason for the ubiquitous blurring of entertainment and politics, image and reality, is that Washington politics "often plays out in the media as entertainment" (Kilday 2001, 39)—whether as juicy soap-operatic TV-oriented political scandal involving sex, lies, and a stained blue dress or the suspenseful 2000 Florida election featuring judges obliged to political patronage, which was subsequently made into the HBO movie *Recount* (2008) starring Kevin Spacey. The Internet and rise of cable and satellite television also played a part with the proliferation of voracious media outlets requiring content for a relentless twenty-four-hour news cycle. Whereas mainstream media, often with unquestioned deference, reported on Washington politics, *The West Wing* took a step back to dissect the process of governance. The show took a different direction; as president of NBC entertainment Garth Ancier predicted before the series debuted, "the nation's cynicism about politics might actually help *The West Wing*" (Weinraub 1999a, 5).

When Life Imitates Art

From the beginning, the sense of verisimilitude created by *The West Wing* proved a risky balancing act. Its almost true-to-life fantasy of what it felt like being deep inside the White House often "served to blur the boundaries between TV fiction and Washington reality" (Levine 2003, 42). Often when commentators judged the show, it was on its ability to reflect political reality, holding the series to an almost unattainable standard of authenticity. Sorkin, however, *always* stressed that his prime concern was to entertain, even though he did so with drama rooted in the real. "Creating a sense of reality is really important to me," he said, but added, "the appearance of reality is more important than the reality itself" (quoted in Garron 2000, 101).

Only an illusion, but at times it did feel as if the beltway drama had ripped stories straight from the headlines. Mostly there were echoes, but sometimes the series eerily foreshadowed real life. In "Night Five" (3:14), newspaper editor Leonard Wallace (Carmen Argenziano) approaches C. J. about a former White House correspondent, Billy Price, missing while on assignment in the Congo. C. J. lobbies for his release before discovering that Price has been taken by a group of Mai-Mai (Congolese community-based militia) and killed in an ambush. Originally airing on 6 February 2002, the episode paralleled the plight of *Wall Street Journal* reporter Daniel Pearl—whose fate remained as yet unknown. NBC considered canceling the episode but decided instead to pull only the promotional spot (Starr 2002). Later, in Season Seven, fiscally conservative but pro-choice Republican Arnold Vinick finds himself boxed in by George Rohr (Peter MacKenzie) from the American Christian Assembly over pro-life judicial appointments ("Message of the Week," 7:3). This campaign subplot bore a remarkable resemblance to the hearings being held in Washington at the time, where the Senate Judiciary Committee considered how Samuel A. Alito Jr., Bush's nominee to replace Sandra Day O'Connor on the U.S. Supreme Court, would affect *Roe vs. Wade*.

Aside from these parallels, *The West Wing* felt real because, in part, it sounded real. Part of that alleged authenticity came from the résumés of the writers and consultants. Initially these political experts came from the ranks of the Democrats. Dee Dee Myers, former press secretary for the Clinton administration and the first woman to hold the post, influenced to some extent the C. J. character—"Myers meets Rosalind Russell, maybe with a little Eve Arden thrown in there. Maybe some Maude," claimed Janney (quoted in Barclay 2001). C. J.'s ongoing flirtation with Danny echoed, ever so slightly, Myers's relationship with *New York Times* journalist Todd Purdum, but Myers's experience also influenced plots. In "Lord John Marbury" (1:12), for example,

C. J. ridicules a reporter claiming that Indian troops were moving along the Kashmir border, only to find out later that the story is true—a plot idea that paralleled what happened to Myers in 1994 when America bombed Baghdad after she had briefed to the contrary.

Other Democrats included pollster and strategist Patrick "Paddy" Caddell, as well as former legislative aide to the late senator Daniel Patrick Moynihan, Lawrence O'Donnell Jr. From Season Two, veterans of the Reagan White House, Peggy Noonan (speechwriter) and Marlin Fitzwater (press secretary to Reagan and later George H. Bush) served as consultants, broadening the staff and politically balancing the team. Gene Sperling, economist and former White House chief economic advisor to Clinton (and later to Hillary Clinton during her presidential run), and Frank Luntz, political consultant and pollster, swelled the political ranks for the third and fourth seasons. In Season Five, John Wells brought in more Republicans—Kenneth M. Duberstein, former chief of staff to Reagan, as well as conservative columnist John Podhoretz, who had previously dismissed *The West Wing* as "nothing more or less than political pornography for liberals" (2003, 222–23). Among the writing staff was Eli Attie, former chief speechwriter to Vice President Al Gore. In a story closely paralleling how Will Bailey came to work for the Bartlet administration following an exhausting congressional race in the California 47th ("Arctic Radar," 4:10), Attie, burned out and unemployed after the controversial 2000 presidential election, met with Sorkin. Attie recalls "fortuitous timing" played its part; having been deep inside the drama of the Florida recount, he was given his start as a TV scriptwriter (2010).

Press reporting and media events on real-life politicians engaging with the series further stoked the blurring of reality and fiction. In 2000 *TV Guide* ran a story on *The West Wing* "meets the real thing" (Murphy 2000). Accompanying the article were profiles of cast members meeting their real-life counterparts at the Clinton White House. Notes were compared, facts verified: Maria Echaveste delivered bad news to Washington foes like Josh but without the "hyperbole"; and Loretta Ucelli was "the antithesis of the brooding Ziegler" (ibid., 22). The article also told of Secretary of State Madeleine Albright posing for photographs with the cast in Georgetown's famed O Street. Stories like these were not uncommon, particularly in the early days when the links with the real-life corridors of power were genuine—John Podesta and former chief of staff to Clinton Leon Panetta served as advisors to John Spencer (Burkeman 2003), and Martin Sheen lobbied on behalf of Democratic presidential hopeful Howard Dean. The 2000 presidential election saw the cast, in character, campaigning for the Gore-Lieberman ticket. Appearing on the 2000 Halloween edition of *The Tonight Show with Jay Leno* (NBC, 1992–present), Sheen was seen backstage being handed a *West Wing* script by none other than Al Gore. "Here, it's ready," said the Democratic candidate. (In a twist, Leno appeared as himself talking to C. J. in "20 Hours in L.A." [1:16] at a glamorous Hollywood fund-raiser hosted by Ted Marcus [Bob Balaban].) Gore reunited with Sheen on *Saturday Night Live* in 2002 for a skit wherein the ex–vice president tours the set and refuses to leave the faux Oval Office.

Given that *The West Wing* presented "politics as the last (and certainly the most) honorable profession" (Wolff 2000, 42), with its decent and supremely capable characters driven by a strong sense of duty and purpose, it was little wonder that the show appealed regardless of political affiliations. "Every politician would give his eye-teeth for some of that *West Wing* glamour in their team," wrote Iain Duncan-Smith, former leader of the British conservative party (2004), while two hopefuls in the 2010 U.K. Labour leadership contest, Diane Abbott and Ed Miliband, cited "the incomparable" *West Wing* as their favorite TV show for its "idealism"—four years after the series had left our screens.

Closer inspection of what NBC did with its Emmy-nominated freshman drama in August 2000 offers further insight into the collapsing of clear-cut distinctions between fact and fiction, news and entertainment. On 7, 8, and 9 August, NBC reran four stand-alone episodes, nestled between the Republican National Convention (31 July–3 August) held in Philadelphia, when Bush accepted the nomination, and the Los Angeles–based Democratic National Convention (14–17 August), where the Gore-Lieberman ticket was announced. Furthermore, when the DNC concluded, the *West Wing* film crew immediately moved into the Staples Center to start shooting the following day (Fink 2000). In a final (albeit serendipitous) collusion of reality and fiction, on Wednesday, 13 December, at 9:00 PM, as viewers tuned in expecting to see the scheduled Christmas episode tracing the lingering emotional scars from events at Rosslyn ("Noël," 2:10), they instead found themselves watching another dramatic installment of the 2000 election following the Supreme Court's decision to stop the Florida recount. In an election year, the reruns and its associations reminded viewers of the political and cultural relevancy of *The West Wing,* scheduled as it was quite literally in the middle of this hugely significant constitutional moment.

The West Wing played its own part in collapsing verisimilitude with the real in the 2002 "Documentary Special" (3:19). Reminiscences of working inside Washington power came from real-life luminaries including former presidents Gerald Ford, Jimmy Carter, and Clinton, ex-key political advisors such as Dr. Henry Kissinger, Paul Begala, and David Gergen (advisor to the Nixon, Ford, Reagan, and Clinton administrations), and even deputy chief of staff to George W. Bush, Karl Rove, alongside the show's hired political consultants—including Myers, Noonan, and Fitzwater. Just as the participants recollect what it "feels" like to work inside the real White House, extracts from the series wistfully recall the best of *The West Wing.* As the interviewees offered a hymn to the nobility of public service, the documentary acted as a canticle to the series. Everything remembered was carefully staged around producing a "feeling" for the fundamental truths of the series, creating, in turn, a dense memory-scape involving history, experience, and television. Weaving this archive of lived experience with re-remembering fictional scenes from the show further sought to enhance how this milestone television drama mediated idealism as verisimilitude.

Hail to the Chief: Imagining the Presidency

Nowhere has the critical reception to *The West Wing* been more vociferous than in discussions on the construction of the presidency. Never envisioned as more than a peripheral character, Sheen-as-Bartlet soon made his presence felt—and the spotlight shifted. Chiming in with popular sentiment about Washington politics in the post-Lewinsky era, followed by the trauma of 9/11 and ensuing war on terror, this American president "with a strong moral compass [and] a nimble mind" (Holston 2001b, B2) captured the cultural imagination as no other TV president had done before.

In this fictional White House, staffers served at the pleasure of President Josiah "Jed" Bartlet—a three-term congressman, two-term New Hampshire governor, Noble laureate in economics, devoted father of three daughters, faithful husband to his wife (an M.D. from Harvard and board certified in internal medicine and thoracic surgery), devout Catholic proficient in Latin, and a formidable student of history, American and ancient. He was also a New England patrician with a direct ancestral link to a Founding Father.

> Bartlet: My great-grandfather's great-grandfather was Dr. Josiah Bartlet, who was the New Hampshire delegate representative to the Second Continental Congress. The one that sat in session in Philadelphia in the summer of 1776 and announced to the world that we were

no longer subjects of King George III but rather a self-governing people. "We hold these truths of be self-evident"—They said that "all men are created equal." Strange as it may seem that was the first time in history anyone had bothered to write that down. ("What Kind of Day Has It Been," 1:22)

When Bartlet spoke of history, it was not some token lesson he gave. Rather, he projected a sense that he had internalized the American experience. The Bartlets, whose names Josiah and Abigail, notes Caryn James, "reek of America's Puritan past" (1999b, E6), also further ensured his hereditary entitlement to serve. Above all, Bartlet was a thoroughly decent liberal Democrat, concerned for the less fortunate, able to rustle up chili for his staff ("The Crackpots and These Women," 1:5), and a gun-control stalwart but uncompromising on America's enemies. Of his formidable talents, Abbey says, "You have a big brain and a good heart and an ego as big as Montana. [Laughs.] You do, Jed. [Beat.] You don't have the power to fix everything. . . . But I do like watching you try" ("The State Dinner," 1:7)—and so did the audience.

The way Bartlet moved "through *The West Wing* as a functional, living archive of American political discourse" (Pompper 2003, 27) had media commentators talking of him as a modern presidential Prometheus: Franklin Delano Roosevelt complete with a serious health problem, Harry S. Truman with a sharper mind and more refinement, and John F. Kennedy and Bill Clinton without the sexual impropriety. He possessed the social conscience of Carter and "the homiletic folkiness perfected by Reagan" (Conrad 2000, 2; also Holston 2001b). "He was certainly not George W. Bush—not one bit" (Remnick 2006).

It also helped that Bartlet, played by Martin Sheen, looked right, or, as Michael Wolff put it, "*The West Wing* extends the Reagan model . . . [with] an actor who just plays the president becoming as potent a symbol as the actual president" (2000,

46). Sheen's résumé includes past presidential roles, such as John F. Kennedy (*Kennedy*, 1983), but he is also one of Hollywood's most prominent social activists. Supporting various liberal and environmental causes, Sheen has regularly faced arrest during protest action. As he says, "I love my country. I love it enough to draw attention to the dark parts that are destructive" (quoted in Post Wire Services 1999). It was always a question of character.

Several media watchers, however, also declared that this fictional Democrat president was smug, sanctimonious, and self-congratulatory. Chris Lehmann derided Bartlet for being nothing more than a "two-dimension glyph of implausible virtue" (2003, 215, 216), while Caryn James concluded that the president is "played for maximum hokiness and cracker-barrel wisdom" (1999a, E5) and "with such windbag bluster it's a wonder he ever got a vote" (1999b, E1).

For others, scholars included, the Bartlet presidency represented "America's best image of itself" (Rollins and O'Connor 2003, 13). So mesmerizing, so powerful, so intoxicating was this fictional president that scholars soon busied themselves assessing his presidential legacy. Heather Hayton Richardson contends that Bartlet became more *real* than the actual presidential candidates in the 2000 election in his reification of "idealistic promise" as "both the man and office" (2003, 79). Melissa Crawley argues that the stories "used television to return the president to the public by capturing a feeling about the nation's leader" (2006, 194). Building on similar themes, Trevor Parry-Giles and Shawn Parry-Giles find the series responding to prevailing conditions defining the presidency in the Clinton and Bush years. Given that presidential authority had dwindled since the end of the cold war, as well as the complex role played by television in facilitating the presidency as a media performance, *The West Wing* offered "a presidential hero who mirrors the complexity and contingency of the larger U.S. community and puts forth a complicated narrative of nationalism that amplifies the anxieties and uncertainties of the contemporary United States" (2006, 52).

Jefferson Lives: *The West Wing* as Mediator of the Contemporary Political Mind

The West Wing never took directly from political headlines but, nonetheless, was deeply entangled in the national political imagination. The series articulated political dissent and provided a space for a vibrant conversation steeped in a longer history of liberal intellectualism. Patrick Finn advocates that "Bartlet as president preserves the complexity of the issues, of a respect for intelligent debate, and a commitment to the U.S. Constitution" (2003, 110), while Spencer Downing argues that the liberal vision of the Bartlet presidency is "nothing other than the recognition of America's fundamental values" (2005, 144). "Unapologetically patriotic, [Sorkin] created characters that [took] the Declaration of Independence as a credo and the Constitution as a sacred text" (ibid., 130). For Nathan A. Paxton, the series "reinvigorated an old conversation in American political thought" (2005, 148) concerned with power and duty. Each one is a compelling argument, but it was also *in* the process of crafting debate, and *through* the eloquence of language used to utter it, that the show resuscitated American Enlightenment traditions with articulacy and the powers of argument and analysis driving the narrative—and its politics.

With the Clinton sex scandal fresh in the collective mind, there was a weary public skepticism of politicians and political institutions when the series debuted in the United States. Pundits claimed that public cynicism has much deeper roots extending back to Watergate and the resignation of President Richard Nixon. *The West Wing* flourished in its infancy on its almost utopian vision of the executive branch. The series offered a glimpse of something better, something truer, nobler than the partisan sniping and hairsplitting arguments that plagued the final months of the scandal-ridden Clinton presidency and defined the disputed 2000 election. Even when Bartlet started to look like an "imperial president" (Schlesinger 2004), sanctioning covert action against foreign foes without congressional knowledge, the debate his actions provoked allowed the show to remind the nation of who they were and what they believed. In this fantasy White House, partisan agendas mattered less than a desire for how American political life *should* be conducted. "We hope to show that these conversations take place," Wells said, "that there is more serious thought taking place [in Washington] than the world of [media] soundbites" (quoted in Goodale 2000, 16).

"The way to make it real and the way to make it compelling is to give real full-throated arguments to the issues," claimed Sorkin (Kilday 2001, 40). Maybe so, but Sorkin also understood only too well how words and texts have the force to reform politics, even change government—something Senator Obama also appreciated. *The West Wing* developed a unique political voice. Difficult, complex issues were explained; most were never resolved, but the show did give audiences "a sense of debates in progress" (Pompper 2003, 29). The series placed enormous faith in the abiding power of words to transform American life. Jeff Breckinridge (Carl Lumbly) said it best when, in defending his endorsement of a book supporting slavery reparations, he asks Josh to take out and look at a dollar bill ("Six Meetings before Lunch," 1:18) and observes that "the seal, the pyramid is unfinished with the eye of God looking over it and the words 'annuit coeptis,' 'He (God) favors our undertaking.' The seal is meant to be unfinished because this country is meant to be unfinished. We're meant to keep doing better, we're meant to keep discussing and debating." In this act Breckinridge makes visible the series' finest political aspirations. His words acknowledge the role of rhetoric in the enduring debate about the meaning of American democracy and the task of making it work.

Bartlet leading by the power of words

Debating the *how* and *why* of complex issues is what *The West Wing* did well. For example, the series translated the schismatic cultural wars into dramatic conflict and narrative exposition. As weeks turned into seasons, a sense of this intricate and challenging conversation was given room to unfurl. In the pilot episode senior staffers and the president clashed with members from the religious right. The series embraced discussions of gay civil rights (Roundy 2000), as episodes dealt with hate crimes legislation ("Take Out the Trash Day," 1:13), banning homosexuals in the military ("20 Hours in L.A.," 1:16; "Let Bartlet Be Bartlet," 1:19), and same-sex marriage, in which Josh argues with gay Republican congressman Matt Skinner (Charley Lang) on his anti–gay marriage stance ("The Portland Trip," 2:7). Bartlet delivered a theology lesson to conservative talk radio host Dr. Jenna Jacobs (a caricature of Dr. Laura Schlessinger) for calling homosexuality an abomination ("The Midterms," 2:3), picking up on themes of intolerance already flagged elsewhere in the show. Out on the campaign trail candidates became further caught up in America's culture wars, as *The West Wing* entered the combat zone tackling such divisive topics as stem cell research ("A Good Day," 6:17), intelligent design ("Mr. Frost,"

7:4), and abortion ("The Supremes," 5:17; "The Al Smith Dinner," 7:6). The vigorous debates that ensued offered a weekly exchange over the questions that politics could never hope to resolve—religion and sexuality.

Received wisdom among media commentators had it that the idealistic image of public life initially played well. America was enjoying a period of economic stability, and terrorism seemed but a remote possibility. September 11 changed all that, as terrorist action threw the national psyche into reactionary spasm.

Over twenty-five million viewers tuned in for *The West Wing* special, which replaced what was to have been the third season premiere. Titled "Isaac and Ishmael" (in reference to the two sons of Abraham from the Book of Genesis), the episode written by Sorkin and his staff was the first, possibly because of its privileged position to tell political stories, to react to the terrorist atrocities less than a month after they happened. It aired on Wednesday, 3 October 2001, and featured two intertwined narratives, one centering on Josh, along with his colleagues, speaking to a group of high school students identified as the "Presidential Classroom," and the other concerning the detention and interrogation of a suspected terrorist working at the White House. Subjects covered during the security lockdown included Arab stereotyping and racial profiling, "the salience of the presidency," and "the origins of terrorism, its roots in ancient and contemporary history, and its highly contingent and complex quality" (Parry-Giles and Parry-Giles 2006, 162, 163).

Reaction varied as to how this "storytelling aberration" with its civics lesson about terrorism mediated the real-world conversation already taking place. Eric Mink said the episode revealed that it was possible to debate terrorism "in a sensitive, sensible and intelligent way" (2001), while Noel Holston thought it "more articulate and succinct than what passes for discussion on cable's news channels most nights" (2001a). Still, others felt the episode "did little but make pompous speeches"

(Buckman 2001b), complaining that it was "preachy and self-important" (James 2001). Something else happened, though; or, as Steven Aoun put it: "I'm not sure what you were doing on Tuesday, September 11, but I watched *The West Wing* pale into insignificance" (2002, 185). A sense quickly emerged that the series was no longer relevant and, from a foreign perspective at least, unable "to conceive the complexities of the Middle East in anything other than Western terms" (ibid., 187).

Far from being irrelevant, though, the series did attempt, for better or worse, to give voice to American desires and beliefs at a time when public opinion lurched rightward and sought comfort in traditional core values. It was, however, an entire season before *The West Wing* offered its most powerful and moving response to 9/11. Season Four opened on the reelection campaign trail, with Bartlet visiting Reynolds Air Force Base ("20 Hours in America," 4:1). He spoke with soaring eloquence of telling his grandchildren how he sat with "Kings and Cardinals" and, "one morning in September, . . . got to spend a few minutes with the men and women of Air Wing One." Offering them benediction, he descends the dais to a military rendition of "Battle Hymn of the Republic" and into the White House where news arrives that three pipe bombs had detonated during a swim meet at the fictional Kennison State University, killing forty-four people and wounding over a hundred. This act of domestic terrorism involving troubled teenagers, paralleling the 1999 Columbine High School massacre, moves Sam to write an inspirational speech that the president delivers with evangelical zeal: "More than any time in recent history, America's destiny is not of our own choosing. We did not seek nor did we provoke an assault on our freedom, and our way of life. We did not expect nor did we invite a confrontation with evil. Yet the true measure of a people's strength is how they rise to master that moment when it does arise." He goes on to speak of patriotism and promise in this electrifying sermon about national unity and American values, alluding to the brave men killed or

critically injured running "*into* the fire to help get people out."
As this skilled orator reaches his climax, Bartlet exhorts, "The
streets of heaven are too crowded with angels tonight. . . . This
is a time for American heroes. We will do what is hard. We will
achieve what is great. This is a time for American heroes and
we reach for the stars." Woven into the fabric of this speech
are threads of a familiar U.S. rhetorical repertory (self-determinism, frontier mythologies, manifest destiny, patriotic duty)
infused with new meaning (the folklore of 9/11, firefighters,
and the search for heroes). Redemption is preached with scrip-
tural passion. This is the old-fashioned art of political oratory,
borrowing from other orators who spoke about the meaning of
American democracy, stretching from the farmers who made
revolution to Abraham Lincoln and John F. Kennedy.

Its stories in future seasons provided details—often through
heated debate left unresolved—of political complexities rarely
making it into the news. Against the backdrop of a targeted
roadside bombing in Gaza, Season Six kicked off by grappling
with the intricacies of the Middle East at a time when the war in
Iraq, the invasion of Afghanistan, the Israeli-Palestinian conflict
(with the death of Yasser Arafat in November 2004), and oil and
the war on terror dominated the headlines ("Gaza," 5:21; "Me-
morial Day," 5:22; "NSF Thurmont," 6:1; "The Birnam Wood,"
6:2). In the face of mounting pressure from the Republican
House for military retaliation, and despite starting to lose the
media war for delaying his decision, Bartlet resists the tempta-
tion to bomb Iran ("NSF Thurmont," 6:1). The president insists
that he will not use questionable intelligence as a "pretext to
attack another country we don't happen to like"—offering a
counter-narrative to the real-life invasion of Iraq. Indulging in
a bit more wish fulfillment, the series had the administration
bring Israel and Palestine to the negotiating table, allowing for
discussions on regional security, settlements, the right of return, and Jerusalem ("The Birnam Wood," 6:2). With the 2001
Patriot Act rushed to passage without consultation and a nation

in no mood to hear dissent, to say nothing of the brouhaha caused by Sheen's antiwar activities, *The West Wing* tackled topics few other shows dared touch, to say (for better or worse) what was not being discussed elsewhere.

"Far from the Things of Men": Gender Politics, Contemporary Feminism, and Storytelling in Post-9/11 America

Season Five saw the collusion of family matters with political life as never before. The kidnapping of Zoey, which opened the post-Sorkin years, plunged the series deep into the post-9/11 American experience of power and vulnerability. Susan Faludi (2008) talks provocatively of America's psychological response to 9/11 in *The Terror Dream,* and it could be argued that the baffling plot contradictions of this *West Wing* season were not so much about creative upheavals—after all, the series retained and hired leading creative talent—as about what post-9/11 national storytelling revealed about America. Wells said that he believed the series, "thanks to plot developments Sorkin set in motion, [was] 'more in line emotionally with where the country [was]' post 9/11" (quoted in Holston 2004). Trauma was displaced into the domestic realm, scripted largely as about the loss of a beloved daughter—to her family and the nation. Bartlet had predicted this unimaginable terror in Season One following a barroom incident in which four college guys harassed Zoey and Charlie—and the secret service—stepped in ("Mr. Willis of Ohio," 1:6). The abduction of his daughter on home soil provokes a national/narrative crisis and awakened an unease residing deep in the series' memory. Immediately the Republican cowboy barrels into the White House. Some advisors call for retaliation, others counsel restraint, but the newly anointed president Glenallen Walken thunders: "If Zoey Bartlet turns up dead, I'm gonna blow the hell out of something, and God only know what happens next" ("7A WF 83429," 5:1).

Walken's threat to deploy a nuclear arsenal as biblical retribution for the murder of Zoey reflected what Faludi calls "the
culture-wide desire to measure national male strength by female peril" (2008, 262). The haunting "Sanvean," sung by Lisa
Gerrard, plays over the final three-minute montage of the fifth
season opener, as the personal and political dramas unfold in
parallel. Gerrard's lower contralto vocals structure this deep,
dark, and mournful sequence. The First Family attends a private Catholic mass while President Walken presides over the
military bombing of terrorist training camps in Qumar. Everything evolves at a slow pace, capturing a sense of dazed disbe-
lief and disorientation. When the episode first aired in October
2003, America had already been in Iraq for seven months, and
the darker, more sober aesthetic tone suited the more somber

time. Satellite pictures monitor military progress. Leo is seen
alone in the situation room with a fade to the First Family taking communion. The New England family is humbled and dependent on God. Josh and Donna stop by the vigil being held
outside the White House—with candles, photographs, messages, and flowers reminiscent of the vox populi civic displays
that spontaneously sprang up across New York City in the immediate aftermath of the collapse of the twin towers. Each new
shot finds a different character deep in thought—of anguish,
rage, hope, numbness—accompanied by the sorrowful melody
of "Sanvean." Exemplifying Faludi's argument, this shared national event with its primary actor—the absent female—con-
structs a post-9/11 American mythology of lost innocence, of
a father sacrificing for the nation, and of a vulnerable family
grieving a missing child.

Faludi has spoken of how America as the "last remaining
superpower [was] attacked precisely *because* of its imperial pre-
eminence, [and] responded by fixating on its weakness and in-
effectuality" (2008, 9), and of how this fixation played out in
mainstream media and political discourse featuring masculine
men, helpless women, and "security moms." (It is also worth

remembering that one of the conservative columnists celebrating the rise of "manly virtues" from "the ashes of September 11" was none other than former *West Wing* consultant Peggy Noonan [2001].)

Zoey is soon rescued, snatched back from unseen evil by heroic homeland security forces ("The Dogs of War," 5:2). Her almost immediate return after only three days and three episodes seemed fanciful. It was the story everyone wanted, as if the ordeal could not be allowed to continue for too long. The heroic tale of her rescue concludes with Bartlet addressing the nation. His soaring biblical rhetoric is heard as the camera pans over the bedridden but (thankfully) unviolated female body, her family gathered, while her mother stands with her back to the scene. It evokes at once private grief and public healing—the final shot is of Abbey as silent, stoic matriarch staring out of the window, while her husband comforts the nation on the television behind her. Her anger keeps her away from the White House for weeks, and she finds the government shut down and Josh out in the political wilderness when she finally returns ("Shutdown," 5:8).

Conflict in the Bartlet marriage and an intense focus on domestic matters became, to borrow from Faludi, "enlisted in a symbolic war at home, a war to repair and restore a national myth" (2008, 13). A father escorts his "brave little girl" for a walk in the Rose Garden ("Jefferson Lives," 5:3). The politically gifted daughter, Elizabeth Bartlet Westin (Annabeth Gish), chooses family over a congressional run ("Abu El Banat," 5:9). Media inquisitor Diane Mathers (Kathrin Lautner) encourages the rescued Zoey to tell her story with raw emotion and *without* political opinion ("Separation of Powers," 5:7). Images of the abducted daughter caught in perpetual childhood accompanied the media reports of an innocence forever lost. Another daughter, Dr. Eleanor "Ellie" Bartlet (Nina Siemaszko), delivers an impassioned public statement about the necessity for scientific research to be beyond politics after her publicly funded

National Institutes of Health medical study into the human papilloma virus in Puerto Rican sex workers becomes subject to congressional censure ("Eppur Si Muove," 5:16). The mother appears on PBS to heal a beloved children's TV character and soften her media profile ("Eppur Si Muove," 5:16). The feminizing of this harrowing chapter in the fictional nation's history seemed somehow like a retreat, an "odd mix of national insecurity and domestic containment" (Faludi 2008, 13). *The West Wing* world suddenly became populated with beleaguered men, overprotective mothers, and victimized daughters—and the series' (narrative) shakiness and moments of high melodrama revealed less about creative impasse than a particular American reaction to the post-9/11 world.

That said, from the start, the show's depiction of female independence and women of (political) influence was always defined "by struggles between various feminisms as well as by cultural backlash against feminism and activism" (Heywood and Drake 2003, 2). Amid the banter and flirtation, C. J., along with other smart, accomplished women like Amy Gardner and Mandy Hampton, harked back to the spirited screwball heroines of the 1930s and 1940s played by Rosalind Russell, Katharine Hepburn, and Myrna Loy (Ringelberg 2005). In resuscitating this generic type with her new freedoms and greater gender equality, *The West Wing* spoke eloquently and vividly about the lived messiness of contemporary women's lives in our troubled age of emancipation. This is not to suggest the series *was* feminist, or not feminist *enough*, but that it contained different kinds of feminism, a combination of ideas (second wave, postfeminist, liberal feminism, power feminism, antifeminism) sometimes diametrically opposed to each other.

C. J. may have been the political face of the administration, but the execution of her official political role often proved at odds with her feminism. No better example of this can be found than in "The Women of Qumar" (3:9). C. J. must announce a renewed arms package to the fictional Persian Gulf State known for its mistreatment of women. She is privately incensed and airs her objections. She says to Josh, "In Qumar, when a woman gets raped, she'll generally get beaten by her husband and sons as a punishment. So at some point, we should talk about how to spend the $1.5 billion that they're giving us." Matters come to a head when national security advisor Dr. Nancy McNally (Anna Deavere Smith) is dispatched to talk to her. Barely able to contain her fury, C. J. vents about the political hypocrisy of trading with an "allied" nation that abuses women. Nancy says nothing. It is the price of doing business. She cannot shift policy, and neither can C. J. Gathering herself, C. J. walks into the press room to announce the arms deal. Her reaction has been read as "overly emotional" and about the "ancillary role that women's issues play in presidential politics" (Parry-Giles and Parry-Giles 2006, 80), but it also speaks in general of the uneasy status of feminist politics in American cultural life, in particular "the post-9/11 disappearances of feminist and liberal female voices" (Faludi 2008, 39).

105

The plight of Saudi schoolgirls elicited an uncharacteristic political response from C. J. during a press briefing ("Enemies Foreign and Domestic," 3:19). Voicing her personal opinion about burka-clad women in the Muslim world (paralleling the Bush administration's ever so brief commitment to the issue) unleashes a torrent of hate e-mail, including an explicit death threat that prompts Ron Butterfield (Michael O'Neill), head of White House security, to assign protection. C. J.'s sympathy for the girls, who perished after being prevented from leaving a burning building by the mutaween (religious police) because they were not appropriately dressed, became less about international women's rights than American male chivalry. The storyline involving C. J. and her secret service agent, Simon Donovan, translated "saving" women into a narrative of a vulnerable female requiring a male savior. (Not long after his appearance on *The West Wing*, Harmon was given his own police procedural show, heading an elite team of special agents in the

C. J. and Nancy talk about the women of Qumar

hugely successful post-9/11 homeland security drama *NCIS* [CBS, 2003–present].)

Rules are different for women—or so Abbey claimed. The First Lady shared these thoughts with Amy, C. J., and Donna over several bottles of wine while pondering the loss of her medical license and professional identity ("Dead Irish Writers," 3:16). Abbey bemoans how her career "got eaten." C. J., worse for drink, reminds the First Lady of what she has—a husband and children, a home, and a life. C. J. does not even have a cat. She starts to drift. Amy picks up the threads and lists the health care issues for which Abbey has advocated. Almost without thinking, Donna blurts out, "Mrs. Bartlet . . . you were also a doctor when your husband said, 'give me the drugs and don't tell anybody' and you said 'okay.'" Shocked silence descends over the disrespect from a subordinate—but it is all the more shocking because it is a woman, rather than a man, censuring Abbey. She, and not Bartlet, is punished for concealing the MS; and the accomplished thoracic surgeon and adjunct professor at Harvard Medical School with staff privileges at Boston Mercy and Columbia Presbyterian hospitals is ushered back into the post-9/11 American home, "confined to maternal ministrations" (Faludi 2008, 140) and voluntary work at a local health clinic.

Postfeminism found its strongest representative in Ainsley Hayes. Feminist activism for her was irrelevant; women had equality under the Constitution and no need for the Equal Rights Amendment ("17 People," 2:18). Despite being an accomplished lawyer with a fine mind, and in spite of C. J. telling Toby that calling Ainsley a "blond Republican sex kitten" is sexist stereotyping ("And It's Surely to Their Credit," 2:5), reactions to the associate White House counsel had everything to do with gender. Intern Celia Watson (Alanna Ubach) may accuse Sam of sexism in how he speaks to Ainsley, but she refutes Celia's interpretation ("Night Five," 3:14). This incident speaks directly to feminist debates on understanding the continually shifting nature of oppression (what oppresses one woman might not oppress another), while acknowledging it exists, even though it is not always popular to say so—as Celia found out.

Ainsley embodied a type of female empowerment that rejects feminism but is nonetheless profoundly political. She may have claimed that America was moving in the right direction, but feminist lobbyist and liberal Democrat Amy Gardner took a rather different view. It was not enough for women to feel personally empowered; they required real political clout. Amy lobbied to advance women's issues (health care reform, legislation to combat sex trafficking and sexual abuse). But in pushing forward woman-friendly policy agendas, Amy always became dangerously entangled within the very power structures that she sought to challenge—and was forced to resign on principle at least twice ("Posse Comitatus," 3:22; "Constituency of One," 5:5). Both women "are products of all the different, often contradictory definitions of and differences within feminism" (Heywood and Drake 2003, 3). They represent a generation that grew up with equity but nonetheless fundamentally disagree over what exactly equal rights for women might actually mean.

Later seasons find women achieving far more significant political roles. For example, Evelyn Baker Lang (Glenn Close), a federal judge, becomes the first woman Supreme Court justice ("The Supremes," 5:17). The brilliance of her legal and political mind outweighs any potential doubts over disclosure of an abortion—at least *Roe vs. Wade* is safe in her hands. Commander Kate Harper may only be deputy national security advisor (Nancy remained in post until the end), but she counsels the president on brokering a significant peace deal between Israel and Palestine ("The Birnam Wood," 6:2), and her insight on China secures her place at the Chinese summit ("In the Room," 6:8; "Impact Winter," 6:9).

Most significant of the new appointments was the promotion of C. J. to chief of staff. It seemed an unlikely elevation and, quite frankly, an unbelievable one. Yet in its very improbability, which at some level says something important about the popularity of Allison Janney, this unexpected career bump also represented a kind of wish fulfillment. Given that no woman has ever held that position in any administration, this particular political fairytale speaks of female accomplishment not yet realized. C. J. did the job conspicuously well, but in the end she chooses to go and work for a philanthropic organization, focused on improving infrastructure in Africa, and a life with Danny (resulting in marriage and a child) over advancing her political career in the Santos administration ("Institutional Memory," 7:21). If anything, this resolution of C. J.'s narrative arc promotes the principle of choice associated with liberal feminism. But as a single woman who had placed her career ambition above all else (including romance) for seven seasons, this last-minute denouement betrays a sense that "having it all" for a woman does not quite translate into combining high-stakes presidential politics with family life. Furthermore, and in keeping with the generic logic of the screwball romance adopted by the series, there was also sense that in choosing to work on her relationship with Danny, C. J. made the "right" choice in not letting romance get eclipsed by her career.

Post–Civil Rights and the Politics of Race

Asked in a *TV Guide* interview about how the fiction compares to the real, J. Terry Edmonds, the Sam Seaborn of the Clinton administration, felt that the real White House was far more racially diverse than the fictional one (Murphy 2000, 22). Only one African American appeared in the front title credits although others—chairman of the Joint Chiefs of Staff, Admiral Percy Fitzwallace, and national security advisor Dr. Nancy McNally—had a powerful presence in the Bartlet White House. Charlie Young did not appear until the third episode ("A Proportional Response," 1:3) after the NAACP complained that there were not enough African American characters on the show.

Controversy soon followed as Charlie started dating Zoey. The series weaved anticipated concerns over the interracial romance into the narrative. Leo gently teases the president about his discomfort at the budding relationship ("Lord John Marbury," 1:11). Bartlet grumbles that he should have had his youngest daughter locked away. Leo pauses, and asks Bartlet if he has a racial problem.

> Bartlet: I'm Spencer Tracy at the end of *Guess Who's Coming to Dinner*.
> Leo: Okay.
> Bartlet: Racial problem.
> Leo: I'm just sayin' . . .
> Bartlet: My problem isn't she's white, he's black. It's she's a girl, he's not. To say nothing of he's older than she is.

Bartlet may not have minded, but the hate mail started to arrive: the first thing Bartlet asks Zoey's new secret service agent, Gina Toscano (Jorja Fox), is whether she is aware of the letters ("20 Hours in L.A.," 1:16). Bartlet eventually tells Zoey and asks her not to attend the opening of a new nightclub with Charlie ("The White House Pro-Am," 1:17). Matters come to a head outside the Newseum in Rosslyn when gunmen open fire on the president and his staff ("What Kind of Day Has It Been," 1:22). It soon emerges that the shooters are white supremacists whose target was not the president but Charlie ("In the Shadow of Two Gunmen: Part 2," 2:2). Immediately Toby wants to take advantage of approval ratings and legislate against extremist organizations ("The Midterms," 2:3). He searches for a way to go after hate groups, but his idea for them to register their affiliation with the FBI proves unconstitutional. Frustrated, the communications director talks to the president.

> Toby: Why does it feel like this? [Beat.] I've seen shootings before.
> Bartlet: This wasn't a shooting, Toby. It was a lynching. They tried to lynch Charlie right in front of our eyes. Can you believe it?

Charlie, meanwhile, finds it hard to cope. With echoes of what had happened to his mother, a D.C. police officer shot in the line of duty, he is burdened by feelings of guilt until a chance meeting with Andrew Mackintosh (Alfonso Freeman), from technical support, and his son Jeffrey (Myles Killpatrick). "If they're shooting at you, you know you're doin' *something* right," Mackintosh reassures him. Charlie continues to show up for work, which does not go unnoticed. Lecturing Bartlet about personal courage and political conviction, Leo turns to Charlie as an example to them all ("Let Bartlet Be Bartlet," 1:19).

Over the years, *The West Wing* spoke of the deep wounds of race, class, and ethnic divides. The series debated gun legislation and its effect on the African American community ("Five Votes Down," 1:4), broken treaties with the Munsee-Stockbridge Indians ("The Indians in the Lobby," 3:8), a school vouchers pilot program for poor (primarily black) children in Washington, D.C. ("Full Disclosure," 5:15), and ethnic tensions between Latino and African American communities ("Undecideds," 7:8). On one occasion Toby visits Mark Richardson (Thom Barry), Democratic congressman for Brooklyn and chair of the Black Caucus ("Angel Maintenance," 4:19). Toby is seeking congressional support for a peacekeeping bill, but Richardson will vote for it only if an amendment reinstating the draft is attached. Asking why his country is intervening in equatorial Africa when he is "still waiting for intervention in Brooklyn," Richardson questions why advancement for African Americans remains either a McDonald's uniform or a Marine uniform.

Then, of course, there was Representative Matthew Santos, the Democrat congressman from Texas. Eli Attie explains that "the idea of running the race to succeed Bartlet" as a storyline came from Wells, as did the idea for a Latino candidate who "would represent the sort of next wave of politics, a way for the show to be edgy but also plausible" (2010). Santos only appeared briefly in a few episodes before Attie got to "really launch the character, [and] tell us who [Santos] was and what he stood for, and use [Attie's] own campaign background to show the fine detail of establishing oneself on the political map" (ibid.). As he worked on two scripts devoted to Santos ("Opposition Research" [6:11]; "Freedonia" [6:15]), Attie "thought of Obama." Still only a state senator, Obama was taking the political world by storm. Word was that the senator was something special and Attie got in touch with David Axelrod, Obama's key advisor.

111

> I just called and said: tell me all about Obama. We had a couple of great, long conversations, which played a big role in filling out the Obama character, as I'd been assigned to do. Then, of course, a million more parallels emerged. For example, I was listening to a lot of [Bob] Dylan, so I wrote into "Duck and Cover" [7:12] that Santos loved Dylan and it turned out Obama did too. We didn't know all of this at the time. Fate, perhaps? Or sheer bloody coincidence. (Ibid.)

Youthful, Latino, a rising star, with no money? Now wasn't his time, surely. Like Obama, Santos ran as the post–civil rights candidate. The fictional congressman spoke eloquently of a different America and promised a better future for all its citizens, regardless of race and class. Santos did not want to be defined as the Latino candidate, setting out instead his vision of an America of shared, non-partisan values and transracial national unity.

Yet his candidacy—however inadvertently—brought racial divisions into full view and opened old wounds because identity politics is always political. Entering Super Tuesday, pressure mounts on Santos to oppose a controversial anti-immigrant bill ("La Palabra," 6:18). Eddie Garcia (Castulo Guerra), a prominent Latino community leader, expects Santos to condemn the bill that would make it unlawful for illegal immigrants to hold a driver's license. Santos refuses because he will be known only as the Latino candidate if he does. Later Vinick goes after the Latino vote ("Message of the Week," 7:3), switching his message of the week from homeland security to immigration—border controls, a bill helping illegal immigrants working low-paid jobs, and trade relations with Central America. Santos is thrown off message—and irked. He does not want to be pigeonholed, but still, he should have gone after the issues.

In "Undecideds" (7:8) Santos finds himself in the center of racial tensions after an African American teenager is shot dead by a Latino police officer. He needs to win over the black "undecideds," but a visit to the bereaved family ends in travesty after the secret service stop a family member from entering the house and the grief-stricken father angrily ejects Santos and his team. Santos is vexed at being caught up in the middle simply because he is Latino. He is scheduled to address the black church community but unsure how to reach out to them. In the end, Santos delivers an impassioned, unscripted sermon that turns into a truly redemptive moment. Standing in the pulpit framed by the huge stained-glass window behind him, and drawing inspiration from Dr. Martin Luther King Jr., Santos talks about the continuing reality of racial discrimination and our collective failure to realize the message of nonviolence and reconciliation. Santos (like Obama) epitomized a new generation of leadership, using his rhetorical powers to urge the black congregation to accept responsibility in overcoming racial divisions and move beyond blame and recrimination to find compassion because "it will keep us on the road. And we will walk together, and work together."

Santos's victory was as much to counterbalance the real-life loss of John Spencer as anything else. History had yet to be written, and the Santos victory did seem more like liberal wish fulfillment than centuries of racial hatred wiped away. What was exciting about his ascendancy was how unequivocally positive and uplifting it appeared. Given the prolonged and protracted progress of the modern civil rights movement and how divisive the Republican administration (with its conflicts in Iraq and Afghanistan, war on terror, and mismanagement in

Santos appeals to the Undecideds

the aftermath of Hurricane Katrina) proved to be, the fictional campaign of 2006 had put a Hispanic in the White House. The symbolic power of this narrative gesture spoke powerfully of obstacles overcome—of hope against cynicism—and a reminder of shared American ideals despite differences.

"We Had It Good There for a While"
The West Wing Legacy

Even a show as successful and as groundbreaking as *The West Wing* runs its course. Viewers defected, ratings slid, and a principal actor unexpectedly died before NBC decided to call time on the beltway drama. Thus President-Elect Matthew Santos took the presidential oath, and President Josiah Bartlet left office and returned to his New Hampshire farm for the last time on Sunday, 14 May 2006, at 9:00 PM. With the single word "Tomorrow," the series completed its seven-year run on NBC.

The West Wing remains unique. It is a landmark television show precisely because nothing else quite like it exists—then as now. In 2005, ABC debuted *Commander in Chief*, starring Geena Davis as MacKenzie Allen, America's first female president. But the series went the way of other political dramas. It had a tough time finding an audience, and, with stories mired in the sewer of slimy Washington ambition, it was canceled after only one season. Politics on television returned to where it began, as real news or the subject of TV satirists. American politics operates in a highly mediated realm, where celebrity culture collides with the political and where television satire (particularly on cable, where it has flourished) seems better able to provide insight. It may seem a far cry from those early days of *The West Wing* and its soaring rhetoric that spoke of America's highest ideals of democracy, but TV satire like *The Daily Show* shares similar broader ambitions to stimulate a lively civic culture.

I started researching this book at the very moment when the 2008 presidential campaign started to ignite genuine excitement. When *The West Wing* concluded its run in 2006, it did so before a hotly contested presidential campaign between an aging maverick Republican senator from a western state and a Democratic African American outsider. Looking back, the show somehow prophetically predicted the real political contest only two years away. Just as President Bartlet, and later Representative Santos, seduced viewers with oratory of uplift, urgency, and unity, so did a young mixed-race senator from Illinois with his promise to heal a divided, post–civil rights, post-9/11 America. Barack Obama tapped into that side of the nation that sees itself as idealistic and inspirational, a side that for seven years *The West Wing never* stopped talking about.

And then there was Arnold Vinick. Never conservative enough for the Republican base, the fictional senator from California fought not only for the presidency but for the very soul of his party. Like that of Senator John McCain, Vinick's legacy seemed to be that of kingmaker to an obscure socially conservative governor able to energize the party base in ways that he could never hope to do ("Institutional Memory," 7:21). However, the fictional West Virginia governor Ray Sullivan (Brett Cullen) always seemed more plausible than the real-life forty-four-year-old mother of five from Alaska. It did not take long after McCain named Sarah Palin as his running mate, to the bewilderment of political observers everywhere, for her to start dominating the headlines with stories involving abuses of power and an unmarried seventeen-year-old daughter five months pregnant by her high school boyfriend. The Republican PR machinery sprang into action, turning an unplanned teen pregnancy into a political testimony of Palin's pro-life convictions. As U.K. journalist Jonathan Freedland shrewdly observed, "A race that began as *The West Wing* now looks alarmingly like *Desperate Housewives*" (2008, 27). It may have been just another day in the polarized and partisan life of Palin, but it reminds us of what *The West Wing* never let us forget: namely, America remains deeply embroiled in its culture wars.

Michael Wolff claimed that "*The West Wing* could well earn a historic place in the reinvention of political culture" (2000, 44). Of course the victory of Obama at the ballot box took decades to cultivate, beginning with the legacy of civil rights. But somehow *The West Wing* paved the way for how we have come to *read* the machinations of political power, as well as how we expect our politics to "look" and sound. Nancy Franklin said it best when she observed that the series "may not be realistic, but it feels real, and it feels right—if this isn't what the White House is like, it's what it *should* be like" (2000, 290). Just as Bartlet commanded American rhetoric, so did Obama. Just as Santos promised to transcend partisan rancor and expunge the blemish of slavery, so did Obama. *In* and *through* oratory, politics, and aesthetics, *The West Wing* kept alive the history and destiny of the American experience, which is what mattered most.

At its height *The West Wing* was the hottest show on American network television. It undoubtedly brought a new level of sophistication and creativity to primetime. This alone, reflected Noel Holston, was enough to distinguish *The West Wing* legacy. "But [the series] also posited an upbeat, inspiring vision of what a presidential administration could be" (2006, C16). Peter Rollins and John O'Connor refine the point: "In our times, it seems clear that the fundamental attraction of *The West Wing* for Americans is its promise that, despite our failings and lapses, our system is still such a lighthouse. Such an appeal to our better selves is both refreshing and chastening" (2003, 13).

In being asked what he considered the achievement of *The West Wing* for network television, Eli Attie replied: "I'm most proud that it was a show about ideas, about complexity; that it was smart and uncompromising and made no apologies for that" (2010). The series may have offered a vision of a Democratic White House in exile, but its unique contribution was in how it delved deep into America's finest political aspirations, interrogated core values embedded in the Constitution, plundered the best of U.S. cultural values and literary forms, and translated this into contemporary quality network television. Just as the novels of Mark Twain or F. Scott Fitzgerald located a distinct narrative style and form that best talked of the American condition, *The West Wing* owes its milestone status, its distinction as a modern U.S. classic, to how it meditated on the contemporary political and cultural imagination (albeit from a decidedly liberal perspective). The series effected a vibrant conversation about the meaning of American democracy and crafted a distinctive aesthetic style and narrative language, otherwise known as the "Bartlet verse," with which to talk about those ideals. Not a bad presidential legacy.

Chapter 1

1. Mark C. Rogers, Michael Epstein, and Jimmie L. Reeves categorize the eras of the U.S. TV experience, based on economic and technological transformations, as follows: TV1 (1948–75) is defined by centralized network responsibility and with popularity determined "in terms of brute ratings and ruled by the . . . 'least objectionable' programming philosophies" (43); TVII (1975–95) sees the decline of the networks and rise of niche market segments (or narrowcasting) and a "quest for 'quality demographics'" (44); and TVIII (1995–early 2000s) is driven by consumer demand and customer satisfaction as well as shaped by digital technologies and new ways of distribution in terms of program delivery.

Abramson, Steven J. 2007. Thomas Schlamme. *Emmy: Primetime Special*, no. 3, 214–19.

Aoun, Steven. 2002. *The West Wing:* Looking a Gift Horse in the Mouth. *Metro Magazine* 131/132: 184–88.

Attie, Eli. 2010. E-mail interview by the author, 8 June.

Barclay, Paris. 2001. A Woman of Influence. *The Advocate*, 13 February, 41.

Battaglio, Stephen. 2003. Contract Will Extend *Wing*-Span on NBC. *New York Daily News*, 15 January, 75.

Bazin, André. 1972. *What Is Cinema?* Vol. 11. Trans. Hugh Gray. Berkeley: University of California Press.

Bianculli, David. 2000. A Program We Can Support. *New York Daily News*, 6 November, 45.

Bourdieu, Pierre. 1984. *Distinction*. Trans. Richard Nice. London: Routledge and Kegan Paul.

Brunsdon, Charlotte. 1990. Problems with Quality. *Screen* 31, no. 1 (Spring): 67–90.

Buckman, Adam. 2001a. *West Wing* and a Prayer. *New York Daily News,* 15 May, 75.

———. 2001b. *West Wing* Wimps Out on Terror. *New York Daily News,* 4 October, 1.

———. 2006. Decision Day. *New York Daily News*, 6 April, 120.

Bumiller, Elisabeth, with Jim Rutenberg. 2002. *West Wing* Rides Coattails of the Real Thing. *New York Times*, 23 January, A12. http://www.nytimes.com/2002/01/23/us/white-house-memo-west-wing-rides-coat-tails-of-the-real-thing.html?pagewanted=1 (accessed 23 April 2010).

Burkeman, Oliver. 2003. Next Week on *The West Wing . . .* erm. *The Guardian* (*G2*), 7 May, 2–3.

Carter, Bill. 2001a. NBC Searching for Lessons in *Sopranos. New York Times*, 2 March, C1, C7.

———. 2001b. Stringing Together Taut Episodes, Not Codas, on *The Sopranos. New York Times*, 16 July, C1, C8.

———. 2002. Trouble in *The West Wing. New York Times*, 21 October, C1.

———. 2003a. Writer of *The West Wing* Is Resigning from the Show. *New York Times*, 2 May, C2.

———. 2003b. *West Wing* Comes to Terms with GOP. *New York Times*, 24 September, E1, E6.

———. 2006. *West Wing* to West Coast: TV's Auteur Portrays TV. *New York Times*, 11 September, E1, E7.

Cavell, Stanley. 1981. *Pursuits of Happiness: The Hollywood Comedy of Remarriage*. Cambridge, MA: Harvard University Press.

Channel 4. 2005. *More4: The New Adult Entertainment Channel from 4*. London: Channel 4.

Chesterton, G. K. 1922. *What I Saw in America*. London: Hodder & Stoughton.

Cleveland, Rick. 2000. WW Veteran: Rick Cleveland. *Written By*. 1 November. http://b4a.healthyinterest.net/news/000029.html (accessed 5 October 2011).

Combined News Services. 2000. *Wing* Soars to No. 1. *Newsday*, 11 October, A10.

Conrad, Peter. 2000. Hail to the New Chief. *The Observer* (*Review*), 17 December, 1–2.

Crawley, Melissa. 2006. *Mr. Sorkin Goes to Washington: Shaping the President on Television's "The West Wing."* Jefferson, NC: McFarland & Company.

Dale, Peter. 2005. More4 Every Viewer. *The Guardian* (*Media*), 4 April, 11.

de Jonge, Peter. 2001. Aaron Sorkin Works His Ways through the Crisis. *New York Times Magazine*, 28 October, 42–47.

Downing, Spencer. 2005. Handling the Truth: Sorkin's Liberal Vision. In *Considering Aaron Sorkin: Essays on the Politics, Poetics and Sleight of Hand in the Film and Television Series,* ed. Thomas Fahy. 127–46. Jefferson, NC: McFarland & Company.

Duncan-Smith, Iain. 2004. Bartlet, C. J. and Me. *The Guardian* (*G2*), 29 September, 2.

Elber, Lynn. 2001. TV Shows Hum with Walden's Tunes. Associated Press, 5 March. http://www.angelfire.com/tv/onceagain/archives/marc5a.html (accessed 13 May 2011).

Fahy, Thomas, ed. 2005. *Considering Aaron Sorkin: Essays on the Politics, Poetics and Sleight of Hand in the Film and Television Series.* Jefferson, NC: McFarland & Company.

Faludi, Susan. 2008. *The Terror Dream.* London: Atlantic Books.

Feuer, Jane. 1984. *MTM Enterprises: An Overview. MTM "Quality Television,"* ed. Jane Feuer, Paul Kerr, and Tise Vahimagi. 1–31. London: BFI Publishing.

Fink, Mitchell. 2000. Conventional Approach for *West Wing. New York Daily News,* 15 August, 23.

Finn, Patrick. 2003. *The West Wing's* Textual President: American Constitutional Stability and the New Public Intellectual in the Age of Information. In *The West Wing: The American Presidency as Television,* ed. Peter C. Rollins and John E. O'Connor. 101–24. Syracuse: Syracuse University Press.

Franklin, Nancy. 2000. Corridors of Power. *The New Yorker*, 21 and 28 February, 290–92, 294.

Freedland, Jonathan. 2008. Who Knows If Palin Will Bring Victory or Defeat? But the Culture Wars Are Back. *The Guardian*, 3 September, 27.

Friend, Tad. 2001. The Next Big Bet. *The New Yorker*, 14 May, 80–91.

Garron, Barry. 2000. Full Circle. *Emmy* 23, no. 3: 100–102, 104.

———. 2006. Into the West. *Emmy* 28, no. 3: 188–91.

Gehring, Wes. 1983. *Screwball Comedy: Defining a Film Genre.* Muncie, IN: Ball State University.

Gerber, Larry. 2002. Oh Say, Can You See Eye-to-Eye? *Emmy* 312, no. 4068 (23 February): 72–73.

Ginocchi, Francesca. 2010. E-mail interview by the author, 21 May.

Gitlin, Todd. 1994. *Inside Prime Time.* London: Routledge.

Goodale, Gloria. 2000. Acting President. *Christian Science Monitor*, 3 March, 13, 16.

———. 2005. *West Wing* Campaigns for the New President—and Viewers. *Christian Science Monitor*, 1 April, 13.

Graham, Jefferson. 1999. 1 Good Man Trying to Handle 2 Good Shows: Writer Sorkin Adds *Wing* to His *Night. USA Today*, 10 August, 3.

Hayton Richardson, Heather. 2003. The King's Two Bodies: Identity and Office in Sorkin's *West Wing.* In *The West Wing: The American Presidency as Television,* ed. Peter C. Rollins and John E. O'Connor. 63–81.

Syracuse: Syracuse University Press.

Hellerman, Arlene. 2003. A Note from the Editor. *On Writing* 18 (February).

Heywood, Leslie, and Jennifer Drake. 2003. Introduction to *Third Wave Agenda: Being Feminist, Doing Feminism,* ed. Heywood and Drake. 1–24. Minneapolis: University of Minnesota Press.

Hillier, Jim. 1985. Introduction to *Cahiers du Cinéma: The 1950s: Neo-Realism, Hollywood, New Wave,* ed. Hillier. 1–17. Cambridge, MA: Harvard University Press.

Hilmes, Michele. 2003. U.S. Television in the Multichannel Age (Protectionism, Deregulation and the Telecommunications Act of 1996). In *The Television History Book,* ed. Hilmes. 62–67. London: BFI Publishing.

———. 2007. NBC and the Network Idea: Defining the "American System." In *NBC: America's Network,* ed. Hilmes. 7–24. Berkeley: University of California Press.

Hoffmann, Bill. 2000. Sexgate Put *West Wing* off the Air for a Year. *New York Post*, 10 October, 123.

Holston, Noel. 2001a. *West Wing* Tackles Terror. *Newsday*, 3 October, A18.

———. 2001b. *Wing* Clipped by Real-Life Drama. *Newsday*, 17 October, B2–3, B31.

———. 2002. What If *West Wing* Turned Right? *Newsday*, 20 November, B27.

———. 2003. From Left to Right *Wing. Newsday*, 24 September, B2, B27.

———. 2004. A New *Wing* Takes Flight. *Newsday*, 15 January, A10.

———. 2005. Back in the Seat of Power. *Newsday*, 6 February, C16, C21.

———. 2006. Terms of Endearment. *Newsday*, 14 May, C16, C22.

Horan, Dermot. 2010. Interview by the author, 7 May, London.

Huff, Richard. 2002. NBC's Touch of Cash. *New York Daily News*, 5 August, 78.

James, Caryn. 1999a. All the President's Quips: Levity at the White House. *New York Times*, 22 September, E1, E5.

———. 1999b. Does the Mush Keep Brains Afloat on TV? *New York Times*, 15 December, E1, E6.

———. 2001. On *West Wing*, a Twilight World Where Fact Meets Fiction. *New York Times*, 5 October, E26.

James, Clive. 2003. In the Grip of the Eagle. *Times Literary Supplement*, 4 April, 18–19.

Jancovich, Mark, and James Lyons, eds. 2003. *Quality Popular Television:*

Cult TV, the Industry and Fans. London: BFI Publishing.

Johnston, Andrew. 2006. Farewell Address. *Time Out New York*, 11–17 May, 171.

Kaplan, Don. 2001. *Wing* Stars Close to a Deal. *New York Post*, 24 July, 82.

———. 2002. Is *West Wing* Worth $220m a Year? *New York Post*, 18 September, 75.

Kilday, Gregg. 2001. The Two West Wings. *The Advocate*, 13 February, 36–41.

Kitson, Marvin. 2000. This Candidate Has Real Character. *Newsday*, 29 March, B2, B27.

Klein, Paul. 1979. Programming. In *Inside the TV Business,* ed. Steve Morgenstern. 11–36. New York: Sterling Publications.

Kramer, Mimi. 1999. Acting Lessons. *New York Press* (Arts Section), 3 November, 26.

Kuhn, Sarah. 2006. Winging It. *Back Stage East*, 11–17 May, 28–29.

Lambert, Mel. 2000. Insights: Interview with W. G. Snuffy Walden. *Media&Marketing*, December. http://www.mediaandmarketing.com/13Writer/Interviews/MIX.Snuffy_Walden.html (accessed 13 May 2011).

Lehmann, Chris. 2003. The Feel-Good President: The Pseudo Politics of *The West Wing.* In *The West Wing: The American Presidency as Television,* ed. Peter C. Rollins and John E. O'Connor. 213–21. Syracuse: Syracuse University Press.

Levine, Myron. 2003. *The West Wing* (NBC) and the West Wing (D.C.): Myth and Reality in Television's Portrayal of the White House. In *The West Wing: The American Presidency as Television,* ed. Peter C. Rollins and John E. O'Connor. 42–62. Syracuse: Syracuse University Press.

Lotz, Amanda D. 2007. Must-See TV: NBC's Dominant Decades. In *NBC: America's Network,* ed. Michele Hilmes. 261–74. Berkeley: University of California Press.

Lowry, Brian. 2002. *West Wing* Starts Fluttering. *Newsday*, 15 October, B27.

———. 2003. *The West Wing* and a Prayer. *New York Post*, 27 May, S4.

Mayers, Michael. 2005. Focus on *The West Wing. The New Yorker*, 5 December, 33.

McCabe, Janet. 2000. Diagnosing the Alien: Producing Identities, American "Quality" Drama and British Television Culture in the 1990s. In *Frames and Fictions on Television: The Politics of Identity within Drama.* 141–54. Exeter: Intellect.

McCabe, Janet, and Kim Akass, eds. 2007. *Quality TV: Contemporary American Television and Beyond.* London: I. B. Tauris.

Mink, Eric. 2000. *West Wing* Schedule Has Eye on an Election. *New York Daily News*, 8 August, sec. 1, p. 94.

———. 2001. *Wing* Gets It Just Right. *New York Daily News*, 4 October, 112.

Murphy, Mary. 2000. House Call. *TV Guide*, 22 July, 15–16, 18, 20, 22, 24.

———. 2004. Hail to the New Chief. *TV Guide*, 20 October, 8–9.

Murphy, Mary, and Mark Schwed. 2003. Broken Wing. *TV Guide*, 31 May, 37–39.

Noonan, Peggy. 2001. Welcome Back, Duke. *Wall Street Journal*, 12 October. http://online.wsj.com/article/SB122451174798650085.html (accessed 11 November 2011).

Oppenheimer, Jean. 2000. The Halls of Power. *American Cinematographer* 81, no. 10 (October): 74–76, 78, 80–83.

Parkin, Lance. 2006. In the Shadow of Twin Towers. *TV Zone*, 208 (December): 42–44, 46.

Parry-Giles, Trevor, and Shawn Parry-Giles. 2006. *The Primetime Presidency: The West Wing and U.S. Nationalism.* Urbana: University of Illinois Press.

Paxton, Nathan A. 2005. Virtue from Vice: Duty, Power and *The West Wing.* In *Considering Aaron Sorkin: Essays on the Politics, Poetics and Sleight of Hand in the Film and Television Series*, ed. Thomas Fahy. 147–74. Jefferson, NC: McFarland & Company.

Petrozzello, Donna. 2002. TV Pol's Chin Is Up, Even as Polls Drop. *New York Daily News*, 20 November, 87.

Podhoretz, John. 2003. The Liberal Imagination. In *The West Wing: The American Presidency as Television,* ed. Peter C. Rollins and John E. O'Connor. 222–31. Syracuse: Syracuse University Press.

Pompper, Donnalyn. 2003. *The West Wing:* White House Narratives That Journalism Cannot Tell. In *The West Wing: The American Presidency as Television,* ed. Peter C. Rollins and John E. O'Connor. 17–31. Syracuse: Syracuse University Press.

Post Wire Services. 1999. Keeping Sheen out of Jail. *New York Post,* 17 September, 119.

Rayner, Jay. 2005. Wing and a Prayer. *The Observer,* 10 July, 8.

Remnick, David. 2006. So Farewell Then, President Bartlet. *The Guardian* (*G2*), 25 January, 14.

Riley, Jenelle. 2006. Fearless Leaders. *Back Stage East,* 11–17 May, 27, 30, 32.

Ringelberg, Kirstin. 2005. His Girl Friday (and Every Day): Brilliant Women Put to Poor Use. In *Considering Aaron Sorkin: Essays on the Politics, Poetics and Sleight of Hand in the Film and Television Series,* ed. Thomas Fahy. 91–100. Jefferson, NC: McFarland & Company.

Rogers, Mark C., Michael Epstein, and Jimmie L. Reeves. 2002. *The Sopranos* as HBO Brand Equity: The Art of Commerce in the Age of Digital Reproduction. In *This Thing of Ours: Investigating "The Sopranos,"* ed. David Lavery. 42–57. New York: Columbia University Press.

Rollins, Peter C., and John E. O'Connor, eds. 2003. *The West Wing: The American Presidency as Television*. Syracuse: Syracuse University Press.

Roundy, Bill. 2000. The Capital Gang. *New York Blade News*, 8 December, 17.

Ruditis, Paul, and Ian Jackman. 2002. *The West Wing: The Official Companion*. London: Pocket Books.

Schlesinger, Arthur Jr. 2004. *The Imperial Presidency*. Boston: First Mariner Books.

Smith, Greg M. 2003. The Left Takes Back the Flag: The Steadicam, the Snippet, and the Song in *The West Wing*'s "In Excelsis Deo." In *The West Wing: The American Presidency as Television,* ed. Peter C. Rollins and John E. O'Connor. 125–35. Syracuse: Syracuse University Press.

Sorkin, Aaron. 2003a. Introduction to *The West Wing Script Book: Six Teleplays by Aaron Sorkin*. 3–8. London: Pan Macmillan.

———. 2003b. *The West Wing. Seasons 3 & 4: The Shooting Scripts*. New York: Newmarket Press.

Stanley, Alessandra. 2003a. A Whiff of Camelot as *West Wing* Ends an Era. *New York Times*, 14 May, E1, E7.

———. 2003b. A New Regime at the White House. *New York Times*, 24 September, E1, E6.

———. 2004. Will He or Won't He? *West Wing* on Brink of War. *New York Times*, 20 October, E7.

———. 2005. Engrossed in a World of Political Idealism. *New York Times*, 8 November, E1, E8.

Starr, Michael. 2002. *Wing* Airs Pakistan Kidnap Copycat. *New York Post*, 6 February, 66.

———. 2003. Beyond Recognition. *New York Post*, 23 September, 78.

Steinberg, Jacques. 2005. On TV as in Life, Presidents Don't Last. *New York Times* (Arts), 28 January, 1, 7.

————. 2006. On *West Wing*, May the Saddest Man Win the Presidency. *New York Times*, 10 April, E1, E6.

Sternbergh, Adam. 2006. The Aaron Sorkin Show. *New York Magazine,* 18 September, 71–72.

Thompson, Robert J. 1996. *Television's Second Golden Age: From "Hill Street Blues" to "ER."* Syracuse: Syracuse University Press.

Waxman, Sharon. 2001. Not Yet in the Crisis Room, but Close. *Newsday*, 26 July, B2, B3.

————. 2003. Inside *The West Wing*'s New World. In *"The West Wing": The American Presidency as Television,* ed. Peter C. Rollins and John E. O'Connor. 203–12. Syracuse: Syracuse University Press.

Weinraub, Bernard. 1999a. Walking Tall in *The West Wing. New York Times,* 26 September, sec. 13, pp. 4–5, 57.

————. 1999b. For Adults, a Frisson: TV Shows for Grown-Ups. *New York Times*, 28 September, E1.

————. 2000. Leader of the Free World (Free TV, That Is). *New York Times,* 17 October, sec. 2, pp. E1, E8.

————. 2004. *West Wing:* Is It Facing a Struggle to Survive? *New York Times*, 12 August, E1, E8.

Werts, Diane. 1999. Playing It Loose. *Newsday*, 21 September, B27.

————. 2001. Presidential Review. *Newsday*, 16 May, B3, B12.

Wolff, Michael. 2000. Our Remote-Control President. *New York Magazine*, 4 December, 42–47.

Zoller Seitz, Matt. 2001. The President Challenges a Higher Authority. *Star Ledger*, 19 May, 31, 39.